How to
Survive and Thrive
in an **Empty Nest**

Jeanette C. Lauer
Robert H. Lauer

New Harbinger Publications, Inc.

Publisher's Note

This publication is designed to provide accurate and authoritative information in regard to the subject matter covered. It is sold with the understanding that the publisher is not engaged in rendering psychological, financial, legal, or other professional services. If expert assistance or counseling is needed, the services of a competent professional should be sought.

Distributed in the U.S.A. by Publishers Group West; in Canada by Raincoast Books; in Great Britain by Airlift Book Company, Ltd.; in South Africa by Real Books, Ltd.; in Australia by Boobook; and in New Zealand by Tandem Press.

Copyright © 1999 by Jeanette C. Lauer and Robert H. Lauer
New Harbinger Publications, Inc.
5674 Shattuck Avenue
Oakland, CA 94609

Cover design © 1998 by Blue Design
Cover illustration by Ward Schumaker
Edited by Catherine Sutker
Text design by Tracy Marie Powell

Library of Congress Catalog Card Number: 98-68752
ISBN 1-57224-137-3 Paperback

Printed in the United States of America on recycled paper

New Harbinger Publications' Website address: www.newharbinger.com

01   00   99
10   9   8   7   6   5   4   3   2   1

First printing

The nest is empty, but our hearts are full.

To those who help make it happen:

*Jon, Kathy, Julie, Jeffrey, Kate, Jeff, Krista, Benjamin, David,
and John Robert*

Contents

Introduction

Your children are about to leave home. Or they have already left. They may have left because of school, marriage, work in another area, or simply their need to live on their own. In any case, you soon will live in, or already live in, an *empty nest*. You confront once again the fact that life is inexorable change.

Life Is Change—and That's Good

When our daughter was seven years old, we found her weeping softly in bed one night. "What's the matter?" we asked. "We're so happy now," she replied. "I don't want it to change." She was becoming aware of her inability to cling to a happy moment and prevent it from fading into memory. We tried to bring her some solace by reminding her of the recurring happiness brought by good memories and of all the positive things she was going to experience in the future.

If a phase of life has been fulfilling, however, it is difficult to have it end. There are times in each of our lives when things are going so well that we would like to freeze existence and keep everything just as it is. Perhaps the child-rearing years have been like that for you. Perhaps the very words "empty nest" make you shudder. Or maybe you react to them with a flutter of anticipation. Or, like many others, you may alternate between a shudder and a flutter. As we shall discuss in chapter 1, people tend to enter the empty-nest stage with a mix of emotions.

In any case, the empty nest is another part of the inevitable cycle of change in human life. And the message of this book is that change, while often challenging and sometimes painful, is basically good. The words philosopher Alfred North Whitehead (1933, 257) used about civilizations can also apply to our individual lives:

> *But even perfection will not bear the tedium of indefinite repetition. To sustain a civilization with the intensity of its first ardour requires more than learning. Adventure is essential, namely, the search for new perfections.*

This book, then, is a call to *adventure*; adventure of change, adventure of discovery, adventure of growth, and the adventure of "new perfections." We offer you more than merely a call. No adventure is unremitting exhilaration. Adventure also entails struggle. It demands effort, and it requires the mindfulness that sets directions and keeps goals in view. Thus, it is our purpose to give you not only a call to adventure but also a resource enabling you to exploit the riches to be found in the adventure of the empty-nest years.

How to Read This Book

To help you along in your adventure, we've included numerous real life examples. We have changed names and circumstances to protect privacy, but all the examples are based on real life experiences. We suggest that you read the experiences carefully and consider using them in one of two ways. Certain cases may provide you with a model to replicate. In other cases, the examples may stimulate your thinking so that you take a creative direction of your own.

We have also included exercises. There are reflection exercises preparing you for the following section in the book. Others, however, are writing exercises that can be useful to you not only at the moment, but also in the future. We encourage you, therefore, to keep a separate journal or notepad as you read the book. You will want to record the exercises in your journal so that they're readily available for future use. You should also make notes in your journal as you read the real life examples. For instance, jot down anything you might want to think about or any activity you might want to pursue in the future. Make a note of your emotional reactions to what you read. When you've finished this book, and as you progress in your adventure of the empty nest, you'll find it both interesting and useful to go back through your journal. You'll have a record of things you want to do or think about, and a chance to compare how you now feel with how you felt at the time you were reading this book.

Finally, we urge you to read *How to Survive and Thrive in an Empty Nest* from beginning to end rather than in selective portions. You will find that the chapters build on each other. Even if a particular chapter deals with a topic that you think might be of little interest to you at the time, you'll most likely find something useful in it and will be better prepared to make good use of the chapters that follow.

We are aware that if you follow our suggestions—read and reflect upon the examples, do the exercises, keep a journal, and go through the entire book in sequence—it will take some time to read this book. But we believe that the promise of high adventure in this new stage of your life is well worth your time.

Part I

Preparing for the Empty Nest

*I can see now that we began preparing ourselves for
the empty nest from the first years of our children's lives.
I shudder to think how hard it would have been if we
had waited until they were ready to leave.*

—Madeline, a forty-six-year-old
mother of two

1

What Can I Expect?

Your nest is empty. Or it's about to be. The children who have been the focus of your life are carving out their own lives in another place. And you're probably experiencing a mix of feelings—ranging from sadness, emptiness, uncertainty, and loneliness to relief, anticipation, even excitement.

Donna, the mother of three children, has experienced all of these feelings and more. Her youngest son, Kenneth, was the last to leave home. After completing his freshman year at a nearby community college, he applied to a West Coast university—two thousand miles away from home. Several months of tense waiting followed before the university responded to his application. When the letter arrived, Donna remembers that Kenneth just stared for a few minutes at the envelope:

> *It was like he couldn't bring himself to open it. Then he*
> *suddenly ripped it open, read it, and let out a shout of joy.*
> *He'd obviously been accepted. I hugged him and told him how*
> *happy I was for him. I, however, had an awful feeling,*
> *as if something was sucking the very life out of my body*
> *and I couldn't stop it. I was proud of him. I was thrilled*
> *that he was so happy. But I also felt like I was dying. I*
> *hadn't expected to feel this way. My children have always*

*been important to me, but they haven't been the totality of
my life. I have a strong marriage and a rewarding career.
My life is very rich.*

Nevertheless, feelings of despair mingled with the pride and
happiness Donna felt for her son when she realized that her nest
would soon be empty.

Similarly, Frank, a father of four, recalls when his youngest
daughter married and he found himself with an empty nest:

*It was one of the happiest and saddest days of my life. The
wedding was picture-perfect. We were so proud of our
daughter and so thankful for her new husband and for the
family and friends that celebrated this special day with us. But
pride and gratitude weren't our only feelings. As we drove
home from the reception, my wife and I admitted to each other
that we felt miserable about going home to an empty house.*

Take a Moment . . .

to list the expectations you have about the empty nest. That
is, how do you expect the empty nest to affect your life—your emotions, relationships, time, and activities? Include both negative and
positive effects. Keep this list until you have finished this book, then
review and modify it.

The Empty Nest as Trauma

Like Donna and Frank, you may feel a variety of emotions when
faced with an empty nest. In this section, we will help you identify
these feelings and, in later sections, provide suggestions for dealing
with them. Let's begin by looking briefly at the negative feelings—
bewilderment, emptiness, anxiety, grief, and *depression*—before considering the feelings of hopeful anticipation that the empty nest also can
bring.

Bewilderment

"Now what?" The couple who asked this question had lived in
an empty nest for several months. They were struggling with the
focus of their lives now that they no longer had children at home.
Ironically, their bewilderment was intensified because they weren't
experiencing the freedom that they had expected. "When we thought

about the kids leaving home," the wife told us, "all we could think about was the freedom we were going to have. But we don't feel free. What we feel is mostly uncertainty about what to do with ourselves."

Feeling bewildered and unsure about what to do with yourself is a common reaction to the empty nest. It reflects what Eric Berne in his book, *Games People Play*, has called "structure hunger"—the basic need to have your time structured rather than completely discretionary (1964, 1b). And if you're like most parents, the majority of your adult life has probably been structured around the many demands and pleasures of raising children. It's not surprising, then, that you feel bewildered about how to fill your time. Where do you put the hours and energy that went into your children's lives? Until you can answer this question, your sense of bewilderment is likely to continue.

Emptiness

When asked what he thought the empty nest would be like, Greg, a single father whose last child is about to leave home, responded, "Empty and boring." As a single parent, Greg has invested much time and energy in his two sons and has cultivated few friends or interests outside of work and family. "It was really tough when Jimmy left for boot camp last year, and now I dread Zach leaving for college this fall." Greg told us that he's battling episodes of emptiness already in anticipation of this "dreaded event."

You may still feel a sense of emptiness even if you have a spouse. For a few weeks after Kenneth left for college, Donna felt the emptiness each time she came home from work. The fact that her husband was there for her didn't fill the void she felt with Kenneth's absence.

> *I would walk into the house and try to act as if nothing had changed. In some ways, it hadn't. Kenneth's room was the same. Well, except that it was a lot neater. But it was still his room, just waiting for him to come home for holidays and summer break. Still, it was a different house. It was a much quieter place. I missed the noise of my son and his friends. I even missed the loud music that used to irritate me when I was trying to relax or concentrate on work. It was like coming home to a mausoleum and I hated it.*

Such feelings of emptiness are a natural reaction to loss. And they're hard to escape because the evidence of loss is everywhere, such as:

- Your child's friends who no longer drop by

- The piano that no one plays

- The sports equipment in the hallway closet

- The lack of mess around the house

- The doors that no longer bang shut

- The relentless quiet

Anxiety

Feelings of anxiety about the empty nest reflect two concerns: what's going to happen to your life without a child around to parent, and what's going to happen to your child without a parent around to care for him or her. Once you get your own life in order and realize that your child is going to survive, the anxiety will subside.

While it lasts, however, the anxiety can be unsettling. Lewis, a happily married father of three, found Friday and Saturday evenings particularly difficult. These were the nights that his only daughter dated and he always stayed awake until she got home. When she moved out on her own, he still stayed awake and worried. "I knew that she was probably out on a date," he said, "and I wasn't there to make certain that she got home safely." For several months, he said, "I would feel fidgety and find it difficult to concentrate on anything until it was late enough that I was sure she was back in her apartment. Then I would say 'Thank you, God' and settle down.

Grief

We were browsing the Internet when we found a message on a bulletin board from a grieving mother. Her last child at home, a son, was leaving soon to enter the military. The prospect of an empty nest was "overwhelming" to her. She realized that children need to strike out on their own but wondered why it had to be so painful for the parent. She said she didn't want to get stuck in grief. She wanted to let her son get on with his life and to get on with her own. She closed by asking if someone had any words of wisdom for her.

Clearly, this mother was already grieving at the prospect of her son's leaving. Grief—the painful feelings of loss, deprivation, and sorrow—is a common emotion among empty nesters. You may cry, feel lonely, and long for your departed child. It's a natural reaction.

Whenever there is a disruption in an intimate relationship, grief is likely. Humans don't take loss easily or lightly.

Depression

Depression is a part of the grieving process. If you grieve over the departure of your children, you're likely to feel depressed at times. As a forty-nine-year-old father said a week after his son moved to a different city, "I feel depressed. I don't have any sense of purpose. And I don't know how to pull myself out of it."

Psychologist Martin Seligman, in his book *Helplessness: On Depression, Development, and Death,* contends that depression occurs when you believe you are helpless to do anything about a painful situation (1975). That is, whatever you do won't change the situation in a desirable way. If the painful situation is the departure of your child, and if you believe that the only way to alleviate the pain is to restore the child-at-home situation, then you are clearly helpless and vulnerable to depression. However, as we shall show in subsequent chapters, there are many ways to alleviate the pain. More importantly, your goal shouldn't be to merely relieve your pain but to launch yourself on a new adventure in living.

The Empty Nest as Hopeful Anticipation

Hopeful anticipation—a sense that the empty nest is an opportunity for a new adventure in living—is also a common feeling experienced by empty-nesters. Yet we have known parents who faced the prospect of an empty nest with hopeful anticipation but later became discouraged when feelings of emptiness and depression lingered. This is even the case for parents who've had strained and difficult relationships with their children. They may be eager to put this phase of their life behind them. Instead of the relief they expected to feel, however, they find themselves struggling with the loss. Their hopeful anticipation dissipated into a dull routine. They didn't know how to take control of their lives and carve out a new dimension of living for themselves. Fortunately, there are steps you can take to ensure a more positive experience of the empty nest.

If you have hopeful anticipation, even if you're still wrestling with some of the common painful emotions, cling to and nurture it. If you don't have such hope, or if yours has slipped away from you, consider a few of the reasons why your life can become a new adventure in living. For example, think of this free time as an opportunity to grow as an individual by focusing more on your own interests and needs. You can begin to:

- Travel

- Cultivate new friendships

- Pursue hobbies or special interests

- Develop your latent skills or abilities

- Revitalize your marriage

- Find a companion if you're single

We will explore ways to restructure your life in more detail throughout this book. For now let's focus on getting prepared.

The Empty Nest as an Equal Opportunity Loss

We made brief reference in the last section to the fact that the departure of children involves a sense of loss. We will discuss how to deal with this sense of loss in chapter 3. First, we want to address two underlying issues: what do you *lose when your children depart,* and *is the loss harder on fathers or mothers?*

What Do You Lose?

The main reason the empty nest is a loss is that you no longer have daily contact with your children. It's actually a two-edged loss: you lose the intimacy of their presence and you lose a role that has been a central part of your selfhood.

Of course, you won't miss all aspects of their daily presence. You're not likely to miss the arguments, the bad moods, the mess, or having to tell your child for the umpteenth time to do something. But contrary to Shakespeare, it's the good that your children do that remain with you and the evil that is buried out of your memory. So you miss the loving aspects of their presence. "I talk to them often on the telephone," a mother said, "but I still want to touch and hug them and just be able to tell them something on the spur of the moment."

Similarly, Paul, a father of two, who is mainly experiencing the empty nest as a new adventure, still recalls the painful loss of intimacy when his children left home:

> *When our daughter left for college, I grieved because it meant that our family was breaking up. I hadn't really thought about us ever being apart until she began to talk about going away to school. A few years later, our son also left. He and I had always talked a lot and done things together. It was almost unbearable to think about not having him around every day.*

With regard to the loss of role, you'll of course always be the parent of your children. But the nature of your parental role, as we shall discuss in chapters 4 and 5, will change. As long as your children live at home, your parental role is typically one of significant involvement. Moreover, this involvement is frequently a central part of your selfhood.

Thus Maggie, an insightful mother of four, realized what she had lost in terms of her self-concept when her last child left home:

> *Although I worked part-time, my children were the center of my life. It was only after they had left home that I became aware of how much my identity was based on my relationship with them. For instance, I would forego something I wanted to do—like going to a concert with friends—because one of my children had a ball game or some other activity and wanted me to attend. Looking back on these years, I realize that I was happy to say "no" to a friend in order to do something for my children. It was my way of saying "I am first and foremost a mother." But now I have had to raise the question of who I am. I just don't feel like the same person I was when they were all at home.*

Who Hurts More—the Mother or Father?

In this chapter, you've heard from men and women who have experienced the loss of an empty nest. You may wonder who feels the loss most keenly, men or women? Our answer: It depends.

Both fathers and mothers can feel the loss keenly when their nest empties. The severity of the loss depends upon a number of factors including:

- How much of your self you have invested in parenting

- What you have postponed in order to parent
- The nature and quality of all of your relationships
- Whether you're a single parent or one of two parents
- How many other interests and responsibilities you have

For instance, men today may feel the loss more keenly than did men in the past because baby-boomer fathers tend to be more involved with their children than were past generations (Levant and Kopecky 1996). The baby-boomer father was most likely present at the birth of his children. Or he may have given higher priority to time with his children than to advancing his career. Like his wife, a considerable portion of his life may have been structured by the responsibilities of parenting. And while greater involvement has no doubt brought baby-boomer fathers much gratification, it possibly has made the departure of their children more painful.

On the other hand, fathers who have been minimally involved in their children's lives may have a sense of missed opportunity. They are at midlife, their career is firmly established, and they recognize the need for greater intimacy in their lives. And this recognition occurs at about the same time their children leave home. Not surprisingly, these fathers are left with the pain that they have blown a significant chance to know and interact with their children.

Mothers, of course, also feel the pain of the empty nest. In particular, if a mother's life has been wrapped up in her children, she may find their leaving extremely traumatic (Bart 1971; Rice 1990). Moreover, the trauma may last for a considerable length of time. Lucy, a mother of two sons, told a counselor that she would never have wanted them not to marry. But when they did, she felt so lonely for them that she couldn't do anything—look for a job, play bridge with friends, or think of any activity that appealed to her. She had literally made her sons her life. When they were gone, she was immobilized by depression.

Single parents of either sex may also experience the empty nest more intensely because it is even emptier than if one's spouse was present. Furthermore, if you're a single parent, you may have unresolved feelings from the past. This is what happened to Sylvia. For five years she raised two children by herself:

Their father just walked out on us. I did my best to be a good mother and to minimize the pain they felt. There were times when I wanted to scream because of the rage I felt against my husband. But I didn't because I was afraid it would hurt my kids. Now my youngest has left the nest. It brings back some

*of the same feelings I had when my husband left—I'm hurt
and angry and depressed.*

Sylvia felt helpless and hopeless after her children left home. In
her efforts to protect and rear her children, she had never worked
through her hurt over being deserted by her husband. When the nest
was empty, she found herself reliving this painful episode at the
same time that she was struggling to cope with the loss of her children. At present, she is in therapy attempting to sort out the emotional morass in which she finds herself.

In addition to overinvested or single parents, those who perceive their children as leaving home at the "wrong" time also may
feel the loss more intensely. There is a certain rhythm to life, and we
feel more keenly the "wrongness" of something if it occurs outside
the expected rhythm. An extreme example of this is when a child dies
before the parents, or parents die at an early age. These are circumstances that feel just plain wrong.

Maybe you feel your child is leaving home at the wrong time.
You think your eighteen-year-old is too young to enlist in the military, live in a college dorm, or get married. Or perhaps you feel that
your child is not sufficiently prepared for the real world, like the
inexperienced young woman who leaves for New York City to pursue her dream of becoming an actress. Whatever the reason, if you
feel that your child is leaving home at the wrong time, your sense of
loss will likely be greater.

In short, both fathers and mothers experience a sense of loss
when confronted with an empty nest. Who feels it more keenly? It all
depends!

Take a Moment . . .

to reflect on your sense of loss. Just what is it you have lost?
Your losses may include both positive experiences—such as the daily
intimacy you had with your children—as well as missed opportunities—such as the wish that you had spent more time with your children. Do you feel you're experiencing the loss any more or less than
your spouse? Or if you're a single parent, do you think this has any
bearing on how you're feeling the loss?

As you reflect on your losses, remind yourself that other parents
have had similar experiences. You're not alone. And most not only
survived their losses but used them as a stepping-stone to a new, fulfilling way of life. You can do the same.

The Empty Nest as a Personal and Relational Watershed

Watersheds are critical turning points in your life. People react to crises in one of three ways—some become mired in their situation, others cope with the situation, and still others use the situation as an opportunity for growth. For the latter group, the crisis becomes a positive watershed, an opportunity for constructive change. No doubt, the empty nest will change your life. It will challenge who you are, who you will become, and what kind of intimate relationships you will have. However, our hope is that you will turn these challenges into a positive watershed.

Who Are You?

As we noted earlier, although you will remain a parent, the nature of your parenthood will change. You'll have more time and energy to devote to other areas. And one important area is your personal identity—who you are now that the nest is empty. In some ways, being in the empty nest is like being an adolescent again. It asks many of the same questions:

- Who am I?

- Where am I headed in life?

- How will I get there?

- What gives my life meaning?

- What do I feel passionately about?

As Maggie, the mother of four quoted earlier, discovered, you probably won't find it easy to answer these questions:

The immediate advice I received from my friends was to pamper myself and pursue new hobbies. Well, I had hobbies, and I had my share of manicures and massages. And I can tell you that they aren't the answer to what life is all about—at least, not for me. I didn't want to fill my time with busy work. I needed something as fulfilling as being a parent. That meant that I had to find out who I am, what I need, what I want, and what I can contribute to this world now that I'm not caring for my children on a daily basis.

For Maggie, the empty nest was a personal watershed that led to may positive changes. After much soul-searching, she decided to return to college and obtain a degree in elementary education. Today, Maggie has an outlet for her nurturing personality—she is giving a class of twenty-five third-graders the love and attention that she gave her four children when they were growing up.

Like Maggie, your life is now taking a different direction. You are on your way to becoming a different person than you were during the child-rearing years. You can devote yourself to things you didn't have time for while your children were at home. The empty nest, in short, will bring change. The question is, how will you respond to these changes? Will they become a positive watershed for you?

Establishing Your Intimate Relationships

The word "intimacy" denotes sex to some people. But sex is only one aspect of intimacy. You can have sex without intimacy, and you can have intimacy without sex. An intimate relationship is characterized by affection, sharing, and mutual commitment. Spouses, relatives, and friends are all a part of the network of intimate relationships. The kind of intimacy you have with a spouse is obviously different from the intimacy you have with a friend. Yet both help fulfill your need for intimate relationships.

Intimate relationships are not merely the icing on the cake in life. They are a fundamental need from infancy to the end of life. Infants can die if they are completely deprived of the cuddling that is their early form of intimacy. Intimate relationships in childhood are related to increased emotional health in adults (Flaste 1991; Hightower 1990). Adults who lack intimate relationships are more vulnerable to various kinds of emotional illnesses such as depression, and various physical ailments, such as bodily pain, colds, and the flu (Mahon, Yarcheski, and Yarcheski 1993; Rubenstein and Shaver 1982; Waring and Chelune 1983). And the best predictor of personal well-being is the quality of people's relationships (Palisi and Canning 1983).

The empty nest is an opportunity for developing and nurturing intimate relationships. If you're married, the empty nest presents a chance to infuse new life into your marriage. Some of the time and energy lavished on your children can now be devoted to your spouse. Your marriage can take on a new vitality, reminiscent of those heady first years together. Indeed, part of the hopeful anticipation of many couples is that they will have more time together and add new meaning to their relationship.

This is not to assume that your marriage is dull or lacks vitality. Nevertheless, unless you are atypical, your marital satisfaction dipped during the child-rearing years. And worse, if you are like some couples, the empty nest may magnify your marital tension or even result in marital disruption.

There are a number of reasons why marriages often encounter difficulty when confronted with an empty nest. One or both of you may have:

- Changed in ways that make you less compatible

- Taken the marriage for granted and failed to keep romance alive

- Avoided personal growth, making one of you less attractive (or even boring) to the other

- Reached a midlife crisis and believe that a new mate is the answer to nagging personal questions

- Pent-up resentments, which have been put on hold because of the demands of child rearing and now resurface

However, if your marriage is strong, you have the chance to add even more vitality to it. If your marriage is troubled by any of the factors in the previous list, the empty nest can be an opportunity to repair the damage and recapture the love of your early years together. If your marriage is beyond repair (hopefully, neither of you will make this assumption before you've made serious efforts to deal with your problems), you may face the pain of disruption. You'll also have the equally difficult yet invigorating task of building new intimate relationships.

If you're single, you also confront the task of building new intimate relationships. Some single parents develop intimate relationships—close friends and/or significant others—while the children are home. Others decide that they have no time for anything other than work and family. But now things are different. Is this the time to start a serious relationship with a potential life partner? To think about getting married again? Or to develop new and closer friendships?

Your intimate relationships will change because of the empty nest. Some of your existing relationships will become more intense and meaningful. Others may fade away. You may develop new relationships. But they will change! Again, the goal is to turn those changes into positive watersheds. This issue of intimate relationships is so important that we will deal with it more extensively in chapters 8 and 9.

Now What?

As we have suggested, various outcomes occur when you reach the empty nest stage. Depending on the choices you make, you will travel on one of three roads. Remember, one road goes nowhere— you *stay mired in a sense of loss*. On a second road, you work through your grief and then *go back to your usual routine*. On the third road, you deal with the loss and move on to a new and exciting phase of your life.

Mired In Loss

Most parents don't stay mired in loss. It's a self-destructive road. Those who do so for any length of time suffer from what therapists call the "empty-nest syndrome"—lasting grief and depression that prevents the individual from carrying on a normal life (Olson 1993).

Various factors can contribute to a prolonged empty-nest syndrome:

- Identity crisis resulting from role loss

- Anxiety about capacity to function well in anything other than the parental role

- Anxiety about the welfare of the departed children

- Guilt about the adequacy of parenting

- Realization that nothing can be done to alter past mistakes

- Overinvolvement in the children's lives

- Overdependence on children for fulfilling emotional needs

Most parents grapple with one or more of these factors and eventually work through them. Those who are overwhelmed by them, those who feel stuck in loss and barren of hope, need therapy. Otherwise, the empty-nest syndrome may plague their lives and rob them of life satisfaction indefinitely. If you still feel stuck in this phase after reading our book, it might be wise for you to seek professional help.

Stagnating in Your Routine

Most parents, as we said, do not get mired in the loss. Most work through the various vexing emotions. And many then take the second road, which leads them to what we regard as a missed opportunity—life as usual. Perhaps both parents have been working. So now they devote more time to their jobs. In the long run, the departure of their children is only a minor blip in the long-standing routine of their lives. Consider Ted's experience:

> It was really upsetting when our last child left home. Actually, it was more upsetting to my wife than to me. I was bothered by her upset, but I felt it was time for the kids to move on with their lives. I guess the major difference their leaving has made is that we don't have to worry about things like packing lunches, doing extra laundry, or checking their schedules before we make our plans. In some ways, life is a lot easier. I wouldn't say it's much different. It's just easier. At times I miss the kids. But I wouldn't want them back living in our house again.

Ted has what he calls a good marriage. For him, this means that he and his wife don't argue much and have a shared, comfortable interest in a number of leisure activities.

On the surface, Ted and his wife have dealt with the empty nest well. They are together. They're doing well in their work. They maintain regular contact with their children. Still, we would argue that they have missed an opportunity. Instead of working more and filling spare time with meaningless leisure activities, they could have invested themselves in those things that would have led to a positive personal and relational watershed in their lives. They could have taken the third road, the one that leads to a new dimension of living.

Adding New Dimension to Your Life

Those who take the third road, the road that leads to a new dimension of living, are taking advantage of a unique opportunity in life. How often, after all, do you have the opportunity to transform a personal crisis into a positive watershed? How often do you have the opportunity to nurture your own growth, cultivate existing and new relationships, and restructure your life?

In short, we urge you to think of the empty nest not merely as something that you survive or as something you must cope with before getting on with life as usual. Rather we encourage you to view it as a unique opportunity for personal and relational growth. The course that Melanie, a mother of two who has been in the empty nest for some years now, chose, is a good example of how you can seize this chance to enhance your life:

> *For months beforehand and a couple of weeks after my youngest left home, I felt devastated. I knew that worse things could happen, but this seemed like the worst thing that I'd ever experienced. At times I thought that the best years of my life were over.*
>
> *Fortunately, neither my husband nor I were willing to resign ourselves to stagnating in the same old routine. We started thinking about and planning for new things we could do. We've always had a good marriage. But being in an empty nest has given us the opportunity to develop a great marriage. We have more fun together now than ever before, even more than when we were first married.*
>
> *It's been a time of personal growth for me as well. I've had time to read and think and meditate. And I feel that I've grown emotionally and spiritually. I've also volunteered for a number of projects in our community and have even been the leader in some of them. This makes me feel needed, useful, and competent.*
>
> *I guess the bottom line is I've been able to do things that I never felt I had the time for when the kids were home. Because my children are still a central part of my life, I feel like I have my cake and am eating it too. And I'm focusing on enhancing my personal life. It's turning out to be a wonderful time of life.*

Not that there won't be problems. Not that there won't be any darkness—days of anxiety, times of struggle, or moments of disillusionment. Such things are part of human existence. But life also includes light—days of rejoicing, times of triumph, moments of fulfillment. The empty nest, whether your children stay nearby or move to a new area, is an opportunity to carve out a new dimension of living filled with anticipation and accomplishment.

Reflecting and Planning

Remember, the feelings of loss that come with children leaving home has been experienced by millions of other parents. You're not alone. Perhaps as you work through your loss you'll learn something enabling you to help others approaching the empty nest stage of life.

Beyond the sense of loss and the grief, there's the choice of which road to take. How will you choose to fill your time? In subsequent chapters, we shall explore in more detail how to make this time of your life a positive personal and relational watershed so that you're able to enter a new dimension of life. To prepare yourself for this transition, answer as fully and honestly as you can two questions: What would I like to have happen in my life now in terms of my personal growth? What would I like to have happen in my life now in terms of my intimate relationships?

As you ponder your personal growth, keep in mind your desire and/or need for such things as:

- Intellectual development

- Emotional maturity

- Physical well-being

- Spiritual development

- Cultivation or refinement of untapped skills

- New experiences

- Purpose and direction

As you ponder your intimate relationships, keep in mind your desire and/or need for such things as:

- Enhancing quality of existing relationships

- Forming new relationships

- Withdrawing from certain relationships

- Learning interpersonal skills such as assertiveness

- Contributing to the well-being of others

- Being an integral part of a group

Write out your answers in a separate journal. As you read through subsequent chapters, you may want to add to, delete from, or modify in some way your answers.

2

Preparing for
the Changes

We were traveling along a sharply winding road in the hills of southern Indiana when we came upon a crudely made sign: "Are You Prepared to Die?" The sign seemed appropriate to the precarious terrain. We certainly felt more vulnerable on that tortuous stretch of road than we had on the interstate highway. At any rate, whoever erected the sign clearly felt that since everyone must die, everyone should be prepared to deal with death.

We'd like to turn the sign on its head and apply it to the empty nest. Our question is "Are You Prepared to *Live*?" Since every parent must sooner or later face the empty nest, he or she should be prepared to deal with the inherent challenges and possibilities in this new phase of life.

Why Prepare?

Preparing for the empty nest won't eliminate the sense of loss or grief we discussed in chapter 1. So why not just wait and deal with your emotions when your children actually leave? Because *being prepared will help you cope with the separation.* It will also facilitate your journey to a new dimension of life. In fact, preparing is important for you, for your children, and for your relationship with them. If you begin preparing, you can make separating a successful process. When your children leave, you want the experience to have positive results for each of you.

Learning from the Unprepared

One way to underscore the importance of preparing is to look at some unsuccessful patterns of launching. They are unsuccessful because, the parents hold on to negative emotions, the children have problems living independently, and the parent-child relationship is troubled after the children leave. Here we look at two unsuccessful patterns—the pattern of *shocked parents* and of *unprepared children.*

Grown children often do things for which their parents are totally unprepared. Consider, for example, the unmarried daughter who moves into her own apartment immediately after she graduates from high school, the son who chooses to go away to a university that is not as highly rated as the one in his hometown, or the daughter who drops out of college after her freshman year to see the world and find herself. In each case, these children feel ready to make their own decisions and leave the nest. They're ready to venture out on their own. But the parents aren't prepared for the separation. In these parents' minds, the only reason for a child to leave home is marriage or a job in another city.

Occasionally, even marriage or a distant job may be defined by the parents as shocking. A young man in his last year of college and living at home announced to his parents that he planned to marry right after graduation. He wasn't prepared for their response:

> *My father went ballistic. He threatened to disinherit me if I went through with my plans. He said I was too young to get married. He said he would wind up supporting both me and my wife. My mother said I needed to have some experience in the real world before I took such a step. She told me I hadn't dated enough girls to be sure about marrying any one of them.*

In spite of his parents' objections, this young man went ahead with his plans. His parents eventually came to terms with his decision and are now happy with his marriage. Yet they could have made the process much easier if they'd prepared themselves for the reality that their children would eventually leave home.

However, children may believe they're prepared to leave the nest when they're not. Unfortunately, their lack of self-reliance was most likely perpetuated by their parents' behavior. Anne and Lenny have three children, a daughter and two sons. All three graduated from a local university—the daughter with a degree in biology and the sons with degrees in business. All three lived at home while they earned their degrees and continued to do so after graduation. All three had the same story: "There just aren't any jobs out there right now."

It was years before Anne and Lenny's nest was empty. The last child was nearly thirty when he finally moved into his own place. Clearly, these children weren't prepared to leave the nest in their early twenties. Nor were Anne and Lenny prepared to have them leave. Rather than encouraging independence, Anne justified their remaining at home:

> *It wasn't their fault. The economy was in a recession. I didn't want them to go somewhere without first having a job. Besides, they were a great help to me and Lenny. Lenny has health problems, and the children did a lot around the house so he wouldn't have to. I'd be glad to see any one of them come back and live at home again.*

Although they have all moved out of the nest, Anne and Lenny's children, now in their thirties, still have problems living independently. Their daughter, who recently divorced, is considering moving back with her parents. Their two sons are married but have unstable work histories and require periodic financial assistance from their parents.

The Aims of Preparing

When you're prepared for the separation, you can more easily avoid the kind of situations just described. But on a more positive note, you want to prepare for your children's departure in such a way that both you and your children can:

- Function independently

- Maintain a close and rewarding relationship

- Move on to an exciting new phase of life

- Experience the departure without suffering long-term negative consequences

Preparing Your Children

Let's first consider ways to prepare your children so that they can function as *independent adults* and *maintain a meaningful relationship with you*. Many children lack these skills.

Psychologist John Bowlby studied a group of academically and socially competent teenagers who left home for college (1973). At the end of the first year, he found that only half were both behaving as self-reliant, effective students and also experiencing meaningful intimacy with their parents during school vacations. The rest were experiencing problems in adjusting to their altered situation.

How do you prepare your children? First, by giving them responsibilities. These responsibilities should increase as they mature and continue until they leave home. Second, by making the departure a celebration of their competence and transition to a new and exciting phase of life.

Giving Children Responsibility

"The biggest mistake I made with my children," a fifty-seven-year-old mother told us, "was to try to protect them from the struggles I had growing up. I felt that I was never allowed to just be a kid and was determined that this wouldn't happen to my children. And did I ever succeed. I did too much for them and, as a result, really prolonged their adolescence."

Giving children responsibility isn't easy. As you may well know, it's often easier in terms of energy and mental peace to do something yourself than to continually remind your child to do it. Yet taking over responsibilities that your children should assume is counterproductive. You only make it more difficult for them to be responsible adults when they leave the nest.

Among other things, taking on responsibilities and making decisions can help your child:

- Build responsibility into his or her character
- Achieve a sense of competence
- Embrace living independently
- Build interpersonal skills
- Foster a sense of control over life
- Initiate moral development
- Handle freedom responsibly

Note that responsibility involves both tasks and decision making. Even young children can be given some responsibilities. Lisa, the mother of seven-year-old Ian, told us:

> *I let Ian select what clothes he will wear each day. If the colors don't match or he chooses something inappropriate, I explain why and he picks something else. I also insist that he dress himself. He would still let me pick out his clothes and dress him every day if I would do it. But as I tell him, he's old enough to make these kinds of decisions for himself.*

As children grow older, they can make an increasing number of their own decisions. Making certain kinds of choices can help your child get accustomed to taking responsibility for him- or herself. This can include such things as:

- Whether to take music lessons
- Whether to play organized sports
- Which hobbies to pursue
- Which scholastic extracurricular activities to pursue
- How to celebrate birthdays
- How to spend money they earn
- Which college to attend
- What kind of career to pursue
- When it's time to leave the nest

Allowing your children to make some important decisions also helps you get used to their being capable individuals. This too can help ease the pain of separation. Of course, you can provide input into the decision-making process. But ultimately your children must make the choice if they are to prepare for independent living.

We have known parents to insist on a child participating in Little League even when the child had no interest in sports. We have known parents to pressure a child to attend a certain college or pursue a particular major when the child preferred something altogether different. We have known parents who have made their child feel apprehensive and guilty about leaving the nest because they weren't ready to let go.

Naturally, your children won't always make the right decisions—even from their point of view. But neither did you. You can't protect them from mistakes. In fact, they'll learn as much from making wrong decisions as from making right ones. And keep in mind that what you think of as a "wrong" decision may turn out to be the best decision for your child in the long run. This is what Henry, the father of three sons, discovered:

> *When Norm graduated from college, he applied to a number of law schools. His dream was to go to Stanford. He didn't get in. But he was accepted by a number of other perfectly good schools. He told us that he decided to stay out of school, work, and reapply the following year. I thought he was making a big mistake and urged him to go to one of the other schools. But Norm was adamant in his decision.*
>
> *The next year he applied again to Stanford and was accepted. After graduation, he obtained a far better position than if he had gone to any of the other schools. I have to admit that if he had followed my advice, he probably wouldn't be as far along in his career today.*

To be sure, there were risks. Norm might not have been accepted at Stanford when he reapplied. The other schools that had accepted him might also have turned him down a year later. Norm might have regretted his decision. But he also would have learned from this. Fortunately, after giving Norm his best advice, Henry wisely supported his son in making his own decision.

As with decision making, even young children can assume responsibility for tasks and take increasing responsibility as they grow older. Some character-building tasks for which children can be responsible, depending on their age, include:

- Keeping their rooms clean
- Cleaning up the kitchen after meals
- Getting themselves up in the morning
- Being on time for appointments
- Doing their own laundry
- Sending thank-you notes when they receive gifts
- Repairing things around the home
- Grocery shopping and cooking occasionally
- Expressing their own style in clothes or bedroom furniture
- Servicing and cleaning the automobile they use
- Working part-time

Children should also learn to use a credit card, write a check, and budget their money. This doesn't mean that they need to do these things on a regular basis, only that they should know *how* to do them.

Take a Moment ...

to evaluate the extent to which you have given your children various kinds of responsibility. If you believe that you've helped your children to be responsible in making decisions and carrying out tasks, commend yourself and read on. If you believe that your children need to be more responsible, decide on two or three ways that you can give them additional responsibility. Remember that it's never too late to do this.

Making the Departure a Celebration

Give your children a gift. Make their departure a time of celebration. You probably won't feel like celebrating. Nor will they. You may cry. So may they. Yet in the midst of the sadness, let them know that the day of departure is also a celebration of their competence, their courage, and their entrance into an exciting new phase of their lives.

It's okay that your children know you're sad to see them leave. At the same time, they should know you're proud of them, hopeful for them, and confident that they're able to handle life's responsibilities. This sends them on their way assured about their ability to deal with what lies ahead. The poorly prepared child may leave home thinking, "It's terrifying to leave home and go out on my own. I don't know if I can do it. And my parents aren't sure I can do it either." The well-prepared child will leave home thinking, "It's tough, but I believe I can do it. And so do my parents."

What if you haven't given your child increased responsibilities along the way? Can anything be done at the last minute to help a poorly prepared child? We suggest two things. First, have some serious discussions with your child affirming his or her competence for meeting the challenges ahead. Remind your child of his or her past successes and achievements.

Second, admit your failure to give your child responsibilities commensurate with his or her competence. Virtually any parent can say to a child, "If I had it to do all over again, I would ..." Your message might be: "If I had it to do over again, I'd give you more responsibilities to help sharpen your skills and give you the confidence you deserve. You're a very competent person, and I could have done more to let you know it." This is the time to set the record straight.

Preparing Yourself: The Long Term

Hopefully, you've been preparing yourself for the empty nest from the time your children were infants. The empty nest is simply the culmination of your child's gradual growth from dependence to independence. Think about it. You probably left the baby with grandma for the weekend. You sent your child off to kindergarten. You allowed him or her to stay over at a friend's house for the night or go away to summer camp. In each case, you were engaged in the separation process. It's important to use these occasions to practice one of the techniques of long-term preparation: *reframing the times of separation*.

Reframing Separation

If some or all of your children are still at home, you'll have opportunities to practice reframing separation. You probably define times of separation as a loss. And they can be. But you can reframe them into a positive loss. Henry did this when his oldest son, Norm, was seventeen and announced that he wasn't going on the family vacation. Henry recalls:

> *I was stunned. At first, I thought he just didn't like the place we were going. But he was firm about the fact that he would not go—wherever we decided to vacation. He said he wanted to work all summer and spend time with his friends. He told us it would be good for us, too, because he would be there to take care of the house.*
>
> *After I got over being stunned, I began to feel depressed. Family vacations were always the highlight of the year for us. Did this mean that Norm and I would never again have one of those great adventures together?*
>
> *For a while, I kept hoping that Norm would change his mind. But he didn't. So I decided that I would have to think*

about it in a different way or the trip would be spoiled for the rest of us. I kept telling myself four things. First, he was right—it would relieve us of the hassle of finding someone to take care of the house. Second, this would be a great opportunity for him to assume some important responsibilities. Third, this would allow us to give more attention to the other two boys. And fourth, it had to happen sooner or later, so why not accept and make the best of it.

Henry's reframing didn't erase his sense of loss, but it did put it in perspective. He no longer simply felt loss. It was a loss that marked a transition time in life—one that had beneficial as well as painful aspects. Moreover, as Henry discovered, the pain soon dissipated and the benefits remained: "All the boys are gone now. And my wife and I are having a ball. I loved those family vacations, but we are free to go places and do things now that were impossible before."

Giving Time to Your Children Now

Henry spent a good deal of time with each of his sons while they lived at home, making the separation even harder. However, it also kept him from having to deal with something that other parents face: regret or guilt over not having given enough time to their children. If your children are still at home, you can do something about this prospect now. You want to avoid the following feelings expressed by Francisco, a father struggling with his sense of inadequacies as a parent:

I'm in a very demanding business. When my daughter was young, I had very little time at home with her. She was asleep by the time I got home at night. And I left in the morning before she was up. I was a weekend father, and even then I sometimes had to be at the office.

I finally got my business under control and could relax a bit and devote more time to my family. Sadly, this happened just a short time before my daughter left home to attend the university. I thought about all the time I had missed with her, and I bounced back and forth between being angry and depressed.

Francisco went to see his daughter at the university to acknowledge his neglect and to ask for another chance. They have begun to build a better and closer relationship. Yet he still regrets that he missed out on so many experiences during the growing-up years in his daughter's life.

Of course, you can't always defer work and other demands to spend time with your children. But in the long run, you'll remember and cherish meaningful moments with your children far more than the extra hour you put in at the office or cleaning the house. You can't always be at the beck and call of your children; but you don't want to swim in regrets of lost opportunities when they leave.

Maintaining Your Personal Interests

This provides a balance in your life that is crucial to the well-being of you and your children. Spending too much time with your children and becoming dependent on them to fulfill your emotional needs will leave you confronting the empty nest with the trauma expressed by Gail, a single mother:

> *I've been the only parent my daughter has known for most of her life. Six months from now, Emily will graduate from high school and then go off to college. I can hardly bear the thought. She's the best friend I have, we share everything. She's been my whole life for nearly eighteen years. What am I going to do?*

Gail mistakenly thought that she was being a "good" mother because she'd abandoned personal interests and focused on her daughter. Initially, she acted to protect Emily from the fact that her father had walked out of their lives. Then it became a habit, a daily cultivation of the only intimacy and strong interest she allowed in her life.

Although Emily has friends her own age, the departure is going to be difficult for both of them. Emily plans to go away because there's no college in her town that offers the course of study she wants. Whether she'll be able to handle the separation remains to be seen. At this point, neither she nor Gail are adequately prepared.

If Gail had maintained interests—friends, hobbies, or community activities—that were distinct from those she shared with Emily, it would have allowed Gail to sustain separate identities. To be sure, she would still experience a sense of loss when Emily leaves. Yet the loss would not be so overwhelming because her life would include much more than her daughter.

Attending to Your Children Still at Home

If you have more than one child, is it easier to let the first one go because you still have others in the home? Probably not. In fact, when the first one goes it can be a bleak harbinger of future losses to come. Like Henry's redefining experience when Norm announced he wasn't going along on the family vacation, you may feel like your family is breaking apart.

It's easy when you're dejected to let your feelings affect the rest of your family, particularly the children who still live at home. Sibling rivalry can emerge even after one of the siblings is gone. Karen was mourning the departure of her oldest child while at the kitchen sink gazing dejectedly out of the window. The voice of her middle child, Nicholas, broke harshly into the silence, "Come on, Mom. Snap out of it. Matt isn't the only kid you have."

Nicholas didn't realize that his mother was mourning his and his sister's future departure as well as that of his brother Matt. From his point of view, Matt's departure seemed far more important to her than did the presence of her other two children. Karen was grateful to her middle child for the remark. It led to a discussion of how they each felt. It also helped them each to prepare for future departures and the eventual empty nest.

Preparing Yourself: The Short Term

The time grows short. It could only be a year or so until your child departs. In addition to the long-term techniques, there are some useful things to do for short-term preparation.

Using Self-Talk

To prepare yourself emotionally, use the technique of *self-talk* (sometimes called *self-instruction*). Self-talk simply involves reminding yourself of those things that will help you to deal well with a particular situation.

Self-talk can be used in ineffective and even ludicrous ways. A man, for example, a man who is highly anxious about giving a public speech might keep telling himself that he isn't afraid. But it doesn't help to keep telling himself that he's not afraid when he obviously is. Such self-talk is a pointless exercise in verbal denial.

Self-talk is effective when it enables you to keep in mind certain facts and perspectives that help you to cope with a situation. Thus, the man who is anxious about giving a speech might tell himself, "I have a job to do; I will do it the best I can, and the important thing is that I communicate my ideas to the audience rather than make them enjoy or agree with what I say."

If your child is leaving home soon, use some or all of the following as part of your self-talk (insert your child's name in the blank):

- _____ is my responsibility but not my possession.

- It's important for _____'s well-being to be able to function independently.

- My relationship with _____ is going to change, but it's going to be an even better relationship.

- I'm going to share in the joy of _____'s achievements.

- Those achievements can only happen if _____ takes this step.

- This is a loss, but it's also a gain.

- I'm beginning a new phase of my life, a phase that others have found exciting and fulfilling.

You may think of other things to tell yourself that will minimize the pain of loss for you. Use them like the items in the pervious list. Remember, self-talk isn't a synonym for self-deception or denial; it's a way to reaffirm the potential for positive outcomes.

🌿 *Take a Moment ...*

to think about the words and/or thoughts that jump into your mind when you contemplate the upcoming separation. In your separate journal, make two lists. Put "Negative Self-Talk" at the top of one and "Positive Self-Talk" at the top of the other. Without denying the reality of the negative, use the positive words and thoughts to put together some statements that you can use in your self-talk. For instance, if your write "loss" in the negative list, write "opportunity" in the positive list.

Anticipating the Benefits

As you construct statements for your self-talk, try to include two ideas that repeatedly come up among people who have found the empty nest to be a time of adventure; namely, *freedom* and *opportunity*:

With the first wave of feelings, you'll more likely feel deprived rather than free. But as your new life unfolds, you'll revel in the freedom that the empty nest brings. Freedom means more discretionary time as well as fewer demands and responsibilities.

One aspect of freedom is being able to set your own agenda. "Enough time has passed at this point," an empty-nester said, "So that I rejoice in knowing that my day isn't already structured for me by all the things I need to do with and for my children."

Another aspect of freedom is quietness and privacy. If the hush of the house initially reminds you of your loss, you may find yourself learning to love the quiet. "Frankly," a mother reported, "I've found the silence and privacy brings me peace. The pace of my life has gone from crazy to calm. And I love it."

A third aspect is a lowered tension level—an outgrowth of fewer responsibilities. A mother pointed out that she worried about wasting time when her children were at home because she always felt like there was so much that she needed to do. "Now I'm able to relax more," she said. "Instead of rushing from one thing to the next, I can enjoy what I'm doing at the moment." Another mother reported that she no longer worries as much about meals and about keeping the refrigerator stocked with food that neither she nor her husband eats. In fact, they can stock up on food that they prefer but that their kids had always complained about.

Fewer financial demands is another aspect of freedom that many empty-nesters enjoy. If you're paying for your children to attend college, you may find yourself with less rather than more discretionary money in the budget. However, as the following observations indicate, sooner or later most empty-nesters experience greater financial freedom:

Now that we have more money, we've become avid amateur astronomers. We've always been stargazers, but now we're really into it. We have purchased a powerful home telescope and become patrons at our local planetarium.

The children have completed college, and now we can afford to travel. Last year we spent a summer touring the wine country in France, and this year we're going to sail the Greek isles.

When the kids were at home, we usually ate in to save money. Now we eat out whenever we can and have made it a rule to try two new restaurants a month. We've discovered that food is a real adventure.

Additional time, money, and energy, coupled with reduced demands and responsibilities, make the empty nest an opportunity. In essence, it's an opportunity for you to explore new dimensions of life. You can now pursue an adventure or cultivate a new interest or skill that you couldn't do before because of the demands of parenting. We'll give numerous examples in later chapters. At this point, we suggest you start making a list of your dreams—what is it you have wanted to do or try or become? You now may have the opportunity to pursue those dreams.

Cultivating New Interests

For the long term, we suggested you maintain a variety of interests. For the short term, as you anticipate the children leaving, explore and cultivate a few new interests as well. You now have the opportunity to start pursuing your dreams.

For example, if one of your dreams is to travel extensively, get some books or maps and start identifying places where you would like to go. Or if one of your dreams is to paint watercolors, enroll in a class and/or read a book about the techniques. Just take small steps at first if it seems overwhelming, but have some fun with your new time.

Occasionally we hear women say, "But all I ever really wanted to be was a mother." (We've never heard a similar statement from a man—that all he ever wanted was to be a father.) One woman who insisted that motherhood was her prime interest in life claimed that she had tried to develop other interests but found them all tasteless.

Our response was this: You will always be a mother. The nature of your mothering, however, will change. It has to change both for your own and your children's well-being. Other interests may have no appeal to you now because you're grieving your impending loss. Keep trying. Continue to explore new interests. After your last child leaves, pursue those interests again. And keep exploring additional ones. We discuss this issue in detail in chapter 6. Eventually you should be able to take advantage of the multitude of opportunities for fulfillment that exist in this world.

Focus on Your Marriage

In chapter 8 we discuss specific ways to enhance the quality of your marriage. However, the process can begin as you count down the days until your nest is empty. Hopefully, you've been nurturing your relationship with your spouse throughout the child-rearing years. If not, the separation will be more painful for you. The woman who said, "All I ever really wanted to be was a mother" was agonizing over the approaching separation in part because her marriage wasn't strong. As she put it:

> *We were good at working together to raise the children.*
> *We are not very good at meeting each other's needs. Even*
> *if my husband is home, I know I'll feel that the house is*
> *empty without the children. They are what made us a family.*
> *I don't know what's going to become of our marriage.*

Clearly, there are some deep issues in her marriage that the empty nest is bringing to light. If you identify with this situation and the materials in chapter 8 do not assist in rebuilding your marriage, you'll probably need professional help.

If you have a strong marriage, on the other hand, you're likely to find yourself using your new freedom as an opportunity to add a fresh dimension of vitality to your relationship. Many empty-nesters talk about the thrill of a second wind in their marriage:

> *To be honest, I thought that life would be dull without the*
> *kids around. But my wife and I find ourselves having the*
> *best time of our lives. We love doing things with just the two*
> *of us, from gardening on the weekends to going to antique*
> *auctions.*

> *We've had a sexual renewal since the children left. We don't*
> *have to lock doors anymore or wait until the children are out*
> *of the house or asleep. We just make love whenever we want.*
> *It's great.*

> *We're on a second honeymoon. We're free to devote ourselves*
> *to each other. I finally have the time to read my wife's poetry,*
> *and she can see what I've been doing with the art program*
> *on our computer.*

Don't wait until the children are gone to catch a second wind in your marriage. Begin now to think about yourselves as a couple and to plan for exciting new adventures together.

Planning for the Day of Departure

Thus far we've suggested various things to do to prepare for the empty-nest years. You also need to prepare for the day itself—the day that your last child leaves home and officially makes you an empty-nester. Both you and your child will probably feel the pain of separation on that day. But it's often easier to be the one leaving than the ones left at home. The one leaving is off to conquer the world. The ones left are sitting in an empty house. So what are you going to do on that day to minimize the pain and loneliness?

One couple decided that they didn't want to return home immediately after dropping their last child off at college. Instead, they planned a camping trip. After they deposited their daughter in her dorm, they set off for a wilderness preserve they had never before explored. As they later reported, "It was an ideal transition time for us."

The important thing is to not wait until your child leaves to decide what to do. Make plans for the day itself. And remind yourself at the end of that day—"This is the beginning of a new and exciting phase of my life." Let your positive self-talk kick in.

Reflecting and Planning

What have you done so far in terms of preparing you and your children for their departure? Take each of the sections in this chapter and think about steps you've already taken. For example, in the two sections dealing with preparing your children, we focused on giving them responsibility and making their departure a time of celebration. For each of these sections, answer three questions: What have I done so far? What still needs to be done? How will I accomplish what still needs to be done?

Answer the same three questions for each of the sections dealing with your own preparation—both the long- and short-term preparation. If you're married, have your spouse work with you. Make this the first project of a renewed focus on your marriage.

Part II

Meeting the Challenges

The art of living resembles wrestling more than dancing, inasmuch as it stands prepared and unshaken to meet what comes and what it did not foresee.

—Marcus Aurelius

3

Adjust . . . Adjust . . . Adjust . . . and More!

Murphy's Law states: "If anything can go wrong, it will." This "law" humorously points out that life presents people with an endless array of problems. Similarly, the Lauers' Law about the empty-nest stage of life states: "Empty-nest challenges come in a very large package, and the whole package arrives at once." This means that, as an empty-nester, you face the task of making multiple adjustments, and you face them as a whole rather than one by one. You have to make adjustments in your daily routines. You have to adjust to a variety of losses. And you have to adjust to the challenges posed by your stage of life. Let's examine these adjustments first and then consider several tools that you can use to deal with them.

Adjusting to Your Daily Routines

We'll begin with *adjustments in your daily routines* because they're often the easiest to handle. However, there will be many and each one will be a reminder that the nest is empty. In some cases the adjustments will be welcome:

> *We no longer hassle about which television program we're going to watch in the evening.*

> *I don't have to rush home at five every evening to start preparing dinner.*

> *It's so much easier to keep the house clean. We only have to pick up after ourselves now.*

Of course, one parent's relief can be another's regret. Adjustments around the same issues are more troublesome for some than for others:

> *My son and I used to watch* Monty Python *together. It was great fun. After he was gone, I tried watching it on my own. I found out that it wasn't the program that I enjoyed as much as sharing it with my son and hearing his laughter.*

> *It's hard to cook for just the two of us. We generally end up with leftovers that I have to throw away. We can't afford to eat out all the time, but I don't enjoy cooking anymore.*

> *At first I got irritated when I saw the clothes piling up to be taken to the cleaners. And my irritation grew when I realized that my daughter had always taken care of this chore and now I was going to have to do it.*

There are some tasks and hassles, then, that will no longer be a part of your daily routine. Yet others—those that were done by your children—are now your responsibility. You'll have to fit them into your routine, or at least get someone else to help do them.

Adjusting to Your Loss

Adjusting to loss is often more difficult to handle than adjusting your daily routines. In chapter 1 we noted the losses of daily intimacy and parental role, but empty-nesters face other losses as well.

The Loss of Being Needed

Yes, you're still needed as a parent. But not in the same way. A mother reflecting on her sense of loss put it this way:

It just hit me one day. My daughter no longer needs me to pick her up from work. She doesn't need me to help her with her studies. She doesn't need me to help her shop for clothes. She doesn't need me to teach her how to cook. All the things I did for her and taught her—that's all over with now. I was her teacher, her protector, her advisor, and her companion. And she doesn't need this from me anymore.

This mother, like many empty-nesters, even missed the aggravations: "You should be able to sew on your own buttons by now." Or, "I shouldn't have to remind you to do your homework every evening." Although these things were annoying, they underscored that she was needed.

The Loss of Meaningful Activities

There are some activities that are meaningful because they are shared with your children. They're not interesting enough that you'd continue to do them alone without your children.

For example, a father recalled his family's annual tradition of searching for the "perfect" Christmas tree:

Every year on the second Saturday in December we'd spend hours trudging through the lots in our quest for the perfect tree. We joked about the "Charlie Brown" trees we saw, argued over our personal candidate for "tree of the year," and groaned when we had to lug it into the house. It was fun. We missed our annual trek last year for the first time, and I was really bummed.

A mother remembered her family's custom of having Sunday breakfast together:

From the time the twins were small until they left for college, we had Sunday breakfast together. Preparation was half of the fun as we flipped pancakes and invented exotic omelets. It was a time to catch up with each other and a way to stay close. I really miss those Sunday mornings together.

The Loss of Community

When your children are growing up, you're likely to be a part of a community of other parents—friends and neighbors who have children the same age. One of the losses reported by empty-nesters is being a part of a community of parents. You no longer participate in activities such as play groups, the P.T.A., Little League, Scout troops, or prom committees. As a mother put it:

> *I live just a few blocks from the school my daughter attended. We always had other kids around. And we often had parents stay for coffee when they came to pick up their kids. Now I don't know anyone at the school. And even when I read about school activities in our local paper, I don't recognize any names. I don't have a sense of belonging to anything in the way that being a part of the parental community provided.*

Adjusting to Midlife

Most people handle those adjustments related to daily routines successfully. And most people adjust to the sense of loss in a reasonably short time. Adjusting to your life cycle, however, can be more difficult. Most people encounter the empty nest at *middle age—a time of multiple challenges.* For example, in addition to the challenge of successfully letting your children go, you may also face the challenge of caring for aging parents—a topic we deal with in chapter 11.

Moreover, middle age, or midlife, will confront you with a number of important developmental tasks, including the following:

- Accepting the aging process and mortality

- Examining and restructuring your close relationships

- Cultivating and maintaining casual friendships

- Evaluating and restructuring life goals

- Assessing the quality of your life

- Forging new directions

These developmental tasks vary somewhat for men and women. For instance, in the aging process men are more likely to be concerned about their sexual performance while women are more likely to be concerned about their sexual attractiveness. In assessing what's important in life, men usually become more interested in nurturing, while women usually become more interested in achievements and/or new experiences.

At this point, keep in mind Lauers' Law: "Empty-nest challenges come in a very large package, and the whole package arrives at once." Thus, just when you're adjusting to the empty nest, you'll also face the other challenges of middle age.

The Challenge of Aging

"I don't even know when it happened," Sam, a father of two, said with a note of distress in his voice. "I looked in the mirror one day and was startled to see bags under my eyes. I looked again. I must say I didn't feel as old as that person in the mirror looked."

You probably don't need for us to go through the litany of changes in appearance and performance that generally occur in middle age. Like Sam just quoted, you're experiencing them for yourself. Still, it may help to realize that what you're experiencing is typical and that your distressed reaction is common.

Aging is difficult in our society because we idealize youth. Americans spend billions of dollars every year to hold back or deny the aging process—everything from cosmetics to reconstructive surgery. It's okay for you to view your own aging with an initial sense of dismay; most people do. Yet keep in mind that once you've done everything you can to keep yourself physically, mentally, and emotionally fit, the emotionally healthiest course is to accept and celebrate this stage of life.

For many people, one of the more difficult aspects is coming to terms with their own mortality. If young people think they are eternal, middle-aged people know full well that they will die someday. This awareness is heightened by the death of parents and friends. It can even tempt people to make rash decisions, such as the woman who decided to have an affair, "a last fling before I die." She was afraid that she'd missed out on something exotic in life, and in a near panic over her impending death (which was probably at least twenty-five years in the future) decided that she would have an affair for the first time in her life. Certainly, there are far better ways to adjust to the challenge of aging.

The Challenge of Sexual Fulfillment

Marital sex has three important functions: *shared pleasure, enhanced intimacy,* and *reduced tension.* A thirty-year-old married woman told us that she didn't believe any couple could maintain an exciting sex life for more than five years. Must sex become stale by the time a couple is in the middle years? Does it still reduce tension, but fail to enhance intimacy or to be an experience of intense shared pleasure?

Yes and no. Sex becomes stale for some couples. But the young woman was wrong; sex can fulfill the three functions just mentioned throughout a marriage. We studied over three hundred couples who'd been married for fourteen years or more. We found a common pattern in which the sexual relationship either remained strong and meaningful or improved. As a woman married for more than thirty years said, "The sex is better than ever."

The challenge of middle age is to keep sex vital and not let it become stale. It's a challenge because men are often concerned about performance because of a decrease in their sexual drive. At the same time, women are often more sexually demanding—a situation that can increase a man's anxiety about performance.

In other words, both you and your spouse may be at a time in your life when two things are happening. First, your sexual needs are changing and, second, your child-free house gives you an opportunity to develop your sexual relationship in a way not possible before. If the changing needs don't cause too much anxiety, the opportunity can be one of the more exhilarating experiences of your empty nest.

The Challenge of Work

Will work outside the home be more or less important to you now that the children have left home? If you were a mother who stayed home to take care of children, you may now decide to pursue a career or feel compelled to help support your child through college. Or maybe you'd like to work but are now faced with caring for your aging parents.

Were you consumed by work when your children were young but now find yourself burnt out, or at least having doubts about the value of continuing to be immersed in your career? Or perhaps you enjoy your job but find yourself the victim of downsizing.

The challenge of work, then, is to deal with the situation in terms of both your own needs and your aspirations. Unfortunately, your needs and your aspirations may not be compatible with each other. Therein lies the challenge.

The Challenge of Purpose

As we briefly discussed in chapter 1, one of the more vexing questions that you face in midlife is: What is the purpose of my life now? Everyone needs purpose; a reason for being that transcends personal pleasure and pain. A major purpose, motivating and directing parents, is raising their children. Once this task is completed, it's natural to reexamine your life and question what will give you direction in the way that raising your children did.

The Midlife Crisis

The combination of the various challenges stemming from your loss and stage of life can result in a midlife crisis. Both men and women experience the crisis (the wife who decided that she would try to have an affair was in the midst of a midlife crisis). In a full-blown crisis, you may feel crushed by life. This can include feeling confusion about the meaning of your life. Aspects of life that were once meaningful—work, marriage, and family—may seem boring, pointless, or even intolerable. The future seems hazy and bleak rather than filled with hope and promise. This crisis can bring with it the following symptoms:

- Decreased energy
- Increased fatigue
- Difficulty getting out of bed
- Difficulty meeting daily responsibilities
- Hard time concentrating
- Withdrawal, self-isolation, or drug abuse
- Intense attempts to recapture meaning in life
- Breaking up old relationships
- Embarking on a new lifestyle

Those who experience a midlife crisis describe it afterward as a season in emotional hell. Fortunately, most people don't go through a full-blown crisis. Many do have at least a mild version, however. You start to question the meaning of life, struggle with melancholy, and are concerned about changing physical appearance and performance. The way you deal with these issues can set the tone for the rest of your life.

Take a Moment …

to think about the challenges you're facing in addition to the challenge of the empty nest. What do you see as the major adjustments to your life now? How many of the challenges of middle age apply to you? To your spouse? Do you see any signs that you or your spouse may be approaching a midlife crisis? What resources can you draw on to meet these challenges? Keep in mind that resources include everything from books to classes to people.

Guidelines for Adjusting . . . and More

The "more" in the title of this chapter, reflects the point we made earlier—the goal isn't simply to adjust to the challenges but to use them as a stepping-stone to add a new dimension to your life.

Several years ago we researched people's watershed experiences—how they dealt with such things as the death of a loved one, divorce, and physical illness. We were particularly interested in what people did who mastered the crisis and managed to go on to achieve a higher quality of life. From their experiences, we were able to extract a number of principles and guidelines for mastering the crises of life. These are tools that you can use to take on the challenges you face as a middle-aged empty-nester and move on to experience a more enriching life.

Take Responsibility for Your New Direction

Time alone does not heal all things. Without some kind of help, many people don't recover from a traumatic experience simply by the healing power of time. Taking responsibility for yourself entails taking control of your own healing process. It means you will not be passive in the face of your hurt and sense of loss. Don't wait for something to happen or for someone to rescue you, instead become proactive about meeting the challenges and restoring your well-being.

You are responsible for initiating the following:

- Restructuring your parenthood

- Expanding your personal horizons

- Becoming useful to others

- Strengthening your couplehood (if you're married)

- Developing your network of intimate relationships

As you do these things, you will be meeting the challenges as well as elevating your life to a new dimension of living. All of these responsibilities will be discussed in more detail in chapters 4 through 9. We will offer more instruction on ways to handle the challenge of meeting your new responsibilities.

Accept and Affirm Your Worth

Maria, a woman struggling with her sense of worth after her children were gone, said: "When they left, my husband still had his career. But my career walked out the door." It's hard to feel good about yourself or your life when a significant chunk of it walked out the door. You may feel that, now that the children are gone, you aren't worth much to anyone. Or you may feel inadequate to pursue anything other than parenting.

Any assault on your sense of worth is perilous. You must believe in yourself and have a sense of your own merit if you're going to enter a new dimension of life. If you're struggling with a sense of worth, therefore, you can use self-talk to accept and affirm yourself. One or more of the following affirmations can help:

- I have just completed one of the most important jobs in the world, and I have done it reasonably well.

- I am loved by my children. They still need me, and they need for me to be a strong, independent person.

- Every person has attractive qualities. I am an attractive person, and I can further develop my attractive qualities.

- I am a capable person. I used my capabilities to prepare my children for life, and I can use them now for new ventures.

- I am a giving person. I gave of myself to my children; I can give of myself to others and make a contribution to this world.

- Every individual has creative potential. I have creative potential. I can develop my creative abilities and use them to enrich both myself and others.

In addition to self-talk, remember affirmations you've received from others—relatives and friends who value you. You can also use religious faith, if you're so inclined, to remind yourself that you're of inestimable value to God. There are many books on ways to bolster your self-esteem, just look in any bookstore's psychology section.

Finally, you can identify and appreciate your skills. In particular, look at the following categories (we have provided a few examples of skills that fall into each category to stimulate your thinking). For each category, write down both the skills you have and those you think you can develop. We suggest you do this on your own and also ask your spouse or a trusted friend to do the same for you. They may observe some skills that you don't recognize in yourself. Use your final list to remind yourself of your worth, potential, and capacity for pursuing new directions in life:

- Interpersonal skills (e.g., good listener; ability to establish rapport quickly; accepting; loyal)

- Physical skills (athletic ability; dexterity; agility; muscular strength)

- Mental skills (e.g, analytical ability; talented debater; can think on feet; can explain things well)

- Aesthetic skills (e.g., gifted musician; artistic; dance well; write poetry)

- Work skills (e.g., dependable; motivated; knowledgeable; work well with others)

- Practical living skills (e.g, gourmet cook, tidy housekeeper; good gardener; capable of making repairs)

- Intimacy skills (e.g, affectionate; verbalize feelings; enjoy sex; affirm others)

Whatever it takes, accept and affirm your own worth. A strong sense of worth is a powerful tool for mastering the many challenges you face. If you believe in yourself, you'll march into the midlife fray with the boldness and confidence necessary to emerge victorious.

Maintain a Focus on Others

When you're cultivating your sense of worth, you're focusing on yourself. This is both valuable and necessary. An entirely self-focused life, however, is destructive. People have known this from ancient times, as illustrated by the story of Narcissus. In Greek mythology, Narcissus falls in love with his own reflection that he sees in a pool of water. Ultimately, he self-destructs from unsatisfied desire and is transformed by the gods into a flower. This poignant myth shows us that too much self-centeredness creates an insidious pattern.

A form of self-focus that afflicts some empty-nesters is *ruminating*—continually brooding on a negative experience—and the negative emotions that accompany it. Ruminating is associated with depression. Ironically, then, the more you chew on a negative experience (as opposed to doing something about it), the less likely you are to deal well with it. Rather, you're likely to find yourself lingering in depression.

One way to get out of a destructive self-focus is to maintain a focus on others. Ask yourself who in your family relations, network of friends, neighborhood, or community could benefit from your attention. If you're married, ask the same question and also consider turning some of your energies to your spouse. Giving yourself to others is part of your purpose in life. And it leaves less time to dwell on your loss or on your own aging.

Focusing on others helped David, a fifty-two-year-old empty-nest father, in meeting the challenge of changing sexual needs. David had begun to worry about his sexual performance:

> For the first time in my life, I couldn't always maintain an erection. And so when I had sex with my wife, I paid more attention to how I was feeling and whether I was erect. That only made matters worse. One day she half-jokingly said to me that good sex wasn't a matter of how you perform but how much you love. What a thought! I started focusing more on her needs after that—on making sex an expression of our commitment and love for each other. And I've had very few problems since then.

Tap Available Resources

An enormous range of resources is available for meeting the challenges. Some are personal. Your willingness to assume responsibility for yourself and to affirm your own worth are important resources.

Other people are also important resources. First, as you reach out to help them, they enrich and give meaning to your life. You once again feel needed and valued. One of the graduate students at the university where we teach did her research and dissertation on altruistic people. That is, people whose careers or pursuits focus on helping others. All of her interviewees reported that they received enormous gratification from helping people. Most of them worked for less money than they would have received in other jobs. Yet, they found the business of helping others so personally enriching that they couldn't conceive of doing something else with their careers.

A second way in which other people become a resource for you occurs in the reverse—you allow others to help you. By doing so, you receive the support you need and they receive the gratification of helping you. If you're struggling with one of the challenges of midlife or with your sense of loss, talk to a trusted friend or relative. Join a support group or form one yourself. There are a lot of people around who are struggling with the same challenges as you are.

Finally, don't forget about such resources as books, tapes, magazine articles, and the Internet. The fact that you are reading this shows that you're aware of the value of books. You might also find self-help tapes or useful magazine articles in your local library. And if you go on the Internet, tell your search engine to look for "empty nest" and you will quickly come up with other empty-nesters eager to share experiences and talk about ways to cope.

Reframe Your Perspective

We noted in chapter two that a useful way of dealing with the anticipation of separation from your children is to reframe your perception. Reframing is also of value in dealing with the empty nest itself and with the other challenges you are facing.

For example, here is how a father, Gary, reframed his midlife concerns about aging:

> *I don't think I paid that much attention to aging as long as the children were at home. Life is pretty hectic with kids in the house. They definitely act as a distraction, consuming an awful lot of your attention and energy. But after the last one left, I began to notice what was happening to myself. One of the first things I remember was digging in my garden and being upset by the fact that my arms tired so quickly. I hadn't noticed that happening before. And then I looked down one day and noticed my bulging middle. I was mortified! When did that happen?*
>
> *I had seen this happen to other men. And I had seen some of them make fools of themselves by trying to pretend it wasn't true. But it is true, it happens to all of us. We grow old. And as I thought about it, I realized that life is a trade-off. Yes, you do lose physically as you age. But you also gain a lot. I think that I have wisdom, the ability to deal with*

things, and a sense of satisfaction that I never had when I was younger. When I hear someone sigh and say "Oh to be young again," my first thought is "Not me! I don't want to be young again. I'd lose more than I could possibly gain."

That's reframing. Reframing occurs when you are able to recognize the complexity of matters and focus on certain aspects rather than on others. As Gary recognized, aging is a complex process. You can choose to focus on what you're losing or on what you're gaining. Gary chose to focus on what he was gaining. He reframed aging from a process of loss to one of growth.

Take a Moment . . .

to practice reframing your perspective. Recall a negative event or challenge you had in the past that didn't work out well. Try to think about it in a positive way. For instance, maybe you hurt someone and even ruined a friendship. You've regretted the incident and subsequent loss. But could it also be viewed as a learning experience that has improved your interpersonal skills? In other words, without denying the mistake you can still appreciate what you learned.

Persevere

When you persevere, you avoid the traps of giving up too quickly and of continuing too long with something that's useless. Consider, for example, the challenge of work. What will you, as an empty-nester, do about working outside the home? Perhaps you're a parent who worked part-time or stayed at home while your children were growing up. What do you do now?

Muriel was a stay-at-home mother. When her last child left home, she took a job as an assistant researcher at the university near her house. She thought that this would help her cope with her deep sense of loss and help fill her empty-nest years. And it did. When she was working, she felt better although there were times when she still felt sad. However, she worked at the job for just four weeks before deciding that the work wasn't going to satisfy her. She abruptly quit. Did she quit too soon? We think so. Staying home again, she began ruminating about her loss, felt depressed, and took much longer to come to terms with her empty nest than if she had persevered in her job.

In contrast, Beth, who had dropped out of school to have children, decided to complete her degree when her youngest went away to college. Like Muriel, she determined that getting a job was the best way to deal with her sense of loss. Since she wanted to teach, she had to finish her degree. This required three years of traveling forty miles back and forth between home and the university. At times when she had to drive on snow-packed roads, she wondered if she'd made a big mistake. Indeed, there were many times when it would have been easier to settle for something less than her dream of teaching. But she persevered, earned her degree, and found great satisfaction in teaching for the next sixteen years.

If, like Beth, you have a dream—something you would really like to do now that you're an empty-nester—persevere in your quest to fulfill that dream. Don't give up too quickly. On the other hand, don't persevere in the pursuit of something that's clearly unattainable. We nearly always encourage people to pursue their educational goals. But we tried to discourage a man who decided that he would like to get an M.D. and become a pediatrician. While he relates well to children, he has no aptitude for science. In fact, he barely passed introductory chemistry as an undergraduate. "Do you realize," we asked him, "that you'll have to take and pass with flying colors a number of advanced science courses before you can even apply to medical school?" Our question didn't faze him. If he perseveres in his dream, he'll invest himself in a quest that will probably end in disappointment. He would do better to persevere with a different dream, one that allows him to dedicate himself to a new career that he resonates with well.

Heighten Your Awareness

From time to time, it's good to be immersed in your own world of thought. You can profitably reflect, plan, and anticipate. However, you also need to get out of yourself and be more aware of what's going on around you. We advise you not to wallow in your depression. You want to avoid preoccupation with thoughts that shut you up in yourself. Open your senses to what is happening around you—heighten your awareness.

As you rise above your sense of loss, you open yourself to new experiences. And new experiences are an important way to celebrate both the empty nest and the aging process. That is, you now have the time to savor new experiences and the maturity to understand and appreciate them in a fresh way. These new experiences can be anything from sensations to observations to interaction with others. Here are examples from two empty-nest parents:

I was sitting on our patio alone, something I rarely had time for before. I closed my eyes and asked myself: "What do I hear?" I identified every sound, including the wind and my own breathing. Then I asked: "What do I feel?" and I experienced things like the breeze against my cheek and the back of the chair pressing gently into my back. The whole experience filled me with a sense of peace and gratitude for the gift of life.

Recently, while we were on vacation, my wife left me in a park while she went off to do some shopping. And I indulged in an afternoon of people-watching. This has become one of my favorite pastimes. I love the variety of shapes and styles that people come in. I love the way they interact with each other. I even like to strike up a conversation with a stranger and learn about his or her life. I've found that there are a lot of fascinating people in this world.

Notice in both examples that the individual wasn't absorbed in his or her own thoughts but was opening up as fully as possible to the environment.

Take a Moment ...

to sense your environment. Practice heightening your awareness. Sit down and open up all of your senses to what's happening around you. What do you see? What do you hear? What do you feel? What do you smell? What does this say to you about your world? Try this exercise when you're alone as well as when you're surrounded by people.

Reflecting and Planning

On separate pieces of paper or in your journal, write down several problems of adjustment that you've encountered as an empty-nester. These can include adjustments related to change in daily routines, feelings of loss, and the demands of midlife. Record how you feel about each of them. In what ways do they require adjustment from you?

Now apply as many of the guidelines we discussed as you can to each of these problem areas. Be as specific as possible. The objective is to construct a plan of action for yourself. For example, if you're experiencing a sense of loss, you might write something like the following:

Sense of Loss

I feel empty and out of kilter with life. I really miss my children and am not sure what to do now. The best way to adjust to the loss would probably be to find something to fill my time and give new meaning to my life. How should I go about doing this?

Take responsibility for your new direction. *This means that I can't expect to just sit and wait for my family or my friends to bail me out. I have to take some kind of action. One thing that might help is to meet some new friends. I can even combine this with my interest in painting. I'll enroll in one of the art classes at the community college this fall and try to meet some new people as well as hone my painting skills.*

And so on. Note the specificity—enrolling in a particular kind of class at a decided time. It does little good to simply say "I have to take action" without specifying the kind of action to take. It does little good to simply say "I need to cultivate new friends" without specifying how you're going to go about doing it. You need to come up with a plan of action.

Do this exercise carefully. Identify the adjustments you need to make. Use the tools. Specify your course of action. And then act.

4

Restructure Your
Parenthood: Needs

A major challenge that confronts you as an empty-nester is how to relate to your adult children. Successfully letting go is only the first step. The next step is determining your future relationship with them. Because the parental role is an important part of your well-being, continued contact is important. In fact, if you're like most parents, continued contact is a certainty. And to some extent, you'll find this continued contact similar to when your children lived at home—sometimes gratifying, sometimes nettlesome, and sometimes a bit of both.

Joan, an office manager with two adult sons, helped her oldest son move into a new office. She enjoyed being with him and helping him. She also found the task wearisome because of her own demanding work schedule. While telling us about the incident, she remarked, "Parenthood is interesting. It's never really over, is it?" "No," we agreed, "you're a parent for life."

Linked for Life

Being linked for life with your children is a cause for celebration—at least most of the time. There will be times, of course, when this lifelong link will distress you. For the moment, however, let's focus on the positive.

Being linked for life is a cause for celebration because an ongoing relationship with your children is probably extremely important to you. Research on parents in the empty-nest stage of life shows that life satisfaction can go up considerably after children leave the home. This occurs especially if there's continued and frequent contact with the children. Of course, what's *frequent* varies from one person to another. The important thing is to have sufficient contact to feel connected with your children in a meaningful way.

There are a number of things that ongoing contact does to enhance your well-being. Among other things, continuing contact:

- Provides you with experiences of love

- Reminds you that you're important to, and needed by, your adult children

- Maintains a certain level of intimacy in your life

- Gives you continued opportunities to nurture

- Enhances your self-esteem and sense of achievement as you watch your children's achievements

- Maintains a sense of continuity with the future

The last point—maintaining continuity with the future—means that in a real sense your influence continues. We were in a museum when we overheard a docent say to a woman who was with her daughter, "As long as she is alive, you will never die." He meant it in a purely physical sense—the daughter looked strikingly similar to her mother. Yet it's true in more than a physical sense. We live on in our children because they carry many of our values and aspirations into a future that lies beyond our limited reach.

Changing the Nature of the Linkage

Given the ongoing relationship with your children, the challenge is to change the nature of your relationship. Namely, you need to learn to relate to your children as adults. In order for this to happen, you must, in the terms used by family therapists, avoid *fusion* and allow *differentiation* to occur. Let's look at the meaning of these two processes and how they affect the quality of your relationship with your children.

Fusion

Everyone has a basic need for intimacy—for relationships of mutual commitment, affection, and sharing. Sometimes, however, people carry the quest for intimacy to the extreme. Instead of relating to each other as two people who retain their individuality, they become like a single, fused person. Their thoughts, activities, beliefs, and even their emotions are indistinguishable from each other.

Fusion in a parent-child relationship can result in such things as:

- The child becomes dependent on your approval

- The child cannot make independent decisions

- The child's reactions mirror the reactions of the parent

- The child's beliefs—including political, moral, and religious beliefs, are identical to the parent's

- The child's aspirations reflect the aspirations of the parent for the child

In other words, adult children in a fused relationship with one or both parents are unable to function as autonomous individuals. They remain in a state of childlike dependence. They may have left their parent's home and stretched the apron strings considerably by distance. But they haven't severed them.

Ironically, a fused relationship, which is often an effort to maintain intimacy, makes a healthy intimacy impossible. Two people cannot relate in a healthy way when one of them is playing God by shaping and controlling the other. You will, of course, influence your children. However, this is quite different from fashioning them according to a mold of your own making. It's great to have a child who is a "chip off the old block" and who will carry something of your own being into the future. It's quite another thing to have a child who can't be distinguished from the "old block."

Differentiation

In contrast to fusion, *differentiation* means that each member of the family becomes an autonomous individual while remaining an integral part of the intimate family group. This may sound paradoxical, but it's a fundamental fact of human life. It reflects what we call the *me-you-we law*: I can only be close to you and speak of "we" as long as I can be separate from you and continue to speak of "me."

We heard a man express well how differentiation supports deep intimacy:

I feel very close to my father. In fact, I can't fully explain my life and the kind of person I am without also talking about him and the kind of person he is. My life is intertwined with his. Yet we are different people in various ways. We don't always agree. We don't share all the same ideas or enjoy all the same activities. But our differences don't negate what I see as an unbreakable, and very meaningful, bond between us.

This man has moved from the dependence of childhood through the independence of establishing his own identity to the interdependence of a healthy relationship with his father. And that's what differentiation achieves—not separation in the sense of alienation, but separation in the sense of autonomous individuals who recognize and practice the interdependence of a healthy intimacy.

Differentiation and Parenting

Differentiation doesn't mean, then, that parenting is over. You aren't like the lower animals who don't even recognize their own offspring. Rather, differentiation means:

- Your children can live without you

- Your children don't want to live without you

- You have fulfilled one of your primary parental responsibilities successfully

When we say that your children can live without you, we mean that they have the skills necessary to get along with other people, uphold a job, maintain their own residence, develop new intimate relationships, and so forth. To say they don't want to live without you means that they want to maintain a relationship with you that may include calling on you for various kinds of help. If your children are at this point, then they have successfully differentiated. And now you're ready to restructure the nature of your parenthood.

✏️ Take a Moment ...

to reflect on your own differentiation from your parents. Before we explore what you and your children need in a restructured relationship, think about your relationship with your own parents. How would you answer the following questions?

- When you left your parents' home, what do you think they still needed from you?

- What did you need from them?

- If you could change anything about your relationship with your parents in the first years after you left home, what would it be?

The questions assume that you had a healthy relationship with your parents. If you didn't have such a relationship with one or both of them, reframe the first two questions in terms of what you wish had been true. The point is, at least some of what you answer is likely to be true for your relationship with your own children. ✏️

What Do You Need from Your Adult Children?

Of course, not everyone needs exactly the same thing. Your needs are probably very different from those of your spouse. Apart from your specific needs, however, you need three general things from your adult children: *continuing contact*, *friendship*, and *affirmation*.

Continuing Contact

How much and what kind of contact you have with your children depends on where they live, what they want, and what you want. If you live in the same area, you're more likely to see each other frequently. But if you're separated by distance, your contact may be limited to occasional visits, telephone calls, letters, or email.

Needless to say, if your adult children live nearby, you're more likely to get caught up in their struggles—marital problems, financial strains, job concerns—than if they lived a thousand miles away. When grandchildren come, you may be asked to baby-sit. You may even find yourself involved in another round of school functions and sporting events—a repeat of what you did with your own children. Some people like this. Some do not.

José and Sandra, for example, are extensively involved with their children and grandchildren. This has yielded them both additional joys and extra pain. Sandra explains:

> *Our kids and grandkids live just a few blocks from us. It's almost like having two nests—one that's empty and one that is chockful. Of course, we don't have to do as much for the grandkids as we did for our kids, but we spend a great deal of time with them. We're at their house or they're over here a couple of times every week. We go places with them and with our kids. This has given us more pleasure than I can tell you. Just being with them has made this one of the best times of life for both José and me.*
>
> *But being so close has its downside, too. Like when our son-in-law lost his job. He really got depressed. Life around their house was pretty grim. And they ran into financial troubles. We even dipped into our savings to help them out. I think we suffered almost as much as they did. But I have to tell you that the good times far outweigh the bad. I wouldn't trade the closeness we have for anything.*

Not everyone is as enthused as Sandra about being so involved with their children and grandchildren. Martin told us a different story:

> *When I retired, I think I shocked my wife when I told her I didn't want to move near either of our children. It isn't that I don't want to see them or know what's going on in their lives. But I don't want to be there and go through every bruise and every fall and every struggle; we did that once, and that's enough.*
>
> *Our daughter has been divorced and is now having troubles in her second marriage. If we lived near her, we would have to deal with this on a daily basis. Besides, she's liable to break up with this husband and move somewhere else. And our son isn't married. So who knows where he'll wind up? I know that he doesn't want to feel like he has to entertain us.*
>
> *Although it was a hard decision for my wife at first, she finally agreed that it's better for us to stay where we are. We can visit our children and they can visit us. And we talk with them frequently on the telephone. I think that's just the right amount of contact to have with your adult children.*

Note that Martin and his wife, like José and Sandra, need continuing contact with their children. But they need less, and a different kind of, contact. As the years go by, the situation may change for both couples. José and Sandra may become less involved as their grandchildren enter adolescence and spend more time with their peers away from family. Martin and his wife may become more involved as their children's lives stabilize.

The point is, you need continuing contact. Yet only you can determine how much and what kind of contact you need. Whether that need is fully realized, of course, depends on your children and their living arrangements, as well as your own preferences.

Friendship

You will always be more than just a friend to your children, but friendship is the core of a restructured relationship. Think about it in terms of what friendship means. A close friendship involves such things as:

- Mutual respect

- Trust

- Keeping in touch

- Sharing feelings, thoughts, aspirations, etc.

- Being available to help

- Emotional support

- Shared experiences

A friendship between you and your adult children should include these factors. Recognizing the importance of these qualities also means that you are no longer the authority figure in their lives. You no longer take the initiative in all matters. No longer are you the source of all knowledge or the final arbiter in all decisions. The unilateral nature of the early parent-child relationship gives way to the mutuality of the adult parent-child relationship. As Kevin, a father of two daughters, expressed it:

I think I first realized that my daughter was an adult when I consulted her about which computer I should buy. I had always thought of myself as the one to give advice to her, to answer questions about everything from school to the afterlife. Suddenly I realized that I was now going to her as she had once come to me. She still asks my opinion. But she also calls my attention to my mistakes, suggests things that I should be doing, and invites me to play golf with her. It's like we've become parents to each other. Or I guess it's more like we've become adult friends.

Friendship increases your ability to enjoy your adult children. As one mother noted: "When my daughter was little, she was nine-tenths worry to me and one-tenth joy. Now she's nine-tenths joy and only one-tenth worry." This reversal occurred because the mother relates to her child as an adult. She's confident that her daughter has the skills necessary to forge her own way in life and, therefore, she no longer feels responsible for her daughter's well-being.

Similarly a father pointed out, "I never realized how enjoyable my children would be as adults. We have great conversations together. I no longer talk *to* them. Now I talk *with* them."

Parents who continue to treat their children as dependents, remaining oblivious to their children's capacity for functioning as adults, deprive themselves of the pleasures of adult children. They also deprive their adult children of the pleasures of relating to parents in a new, more meaningful, and more appropriate way.

Affirmation

We all need affirmation. We need experiences with others that assure us that we're capable, likeable, trustworthy, and so forth. If you relate to your adult children as a friend, you will receive affirmation. Your children will indicate their respect for your opinion, their desire to be with you, and their need for your support. These are the ways that friends affirm each other.

As we noted, however, you'll always be more than just a friend. You also need affirmation as a parent. You need to receive expressions of gratitude for your past efforts and a sense that you're valued and respected now as a parent.

Clearly there are things you can do to keep in touch with, and develop a friendship with your children, but what can you do to receive affirmation? We suggest two things: *recognize* their affirmation and *offer* affirmation.

Affirmation isn't always verbalized. Whenever your children make a request, share something, or treat you in a way that they would not typically do with others, they are affirming you as parent. Make a mental note of those instances and remind yourself that you're special in their lives. Examples include the following:

- You're the only older person included in your child's dinner party.

- Your child calls you first to share the special news.

- Your child introduces you with obvious pride.

- Your child talks to you about unexpected problems.

- Your child wants your opinion on important decisions.

- Your child gets angry in your defense.

If you watch for such things, you may realize that you're getting more affirmation than you thought.

Another effective way to get affirmation is to give it. How much affirmation do you give to your children? Every time you affirm your children, you strengthen and enhance your relationship with them, as well as model desirable behavior. The result, we have found, is that they will reciprocate with their own affirmations.

Unfortunately, we've seen many parents who are more critical or competitive with their children than affirming. We hear such things as:

- You still can't beat the old man, can you?

- You never were very good at that.

- Why don't you come and see me more often?

- What kind of work is that for a woman?

Now think about a more positive, affirming response that could be made in place of each of the putdowns:

- I'm impressed. Your golf game has really improved.

- You're a talented person. Keep trying. You'll get it.

- I'm so glad you came. You always add a glow to my day.

- I'm intrigued—tell me more about your job and what you like about it.

It isn't necessarily true that parents who are competitive with, or critical of, their children lack appreciation or admiration. But they tend to verbalize their competitiveness and critical thoughts and keep their affirming thoughts to themselves. Rather than a dominant theme of affirmation with criticism as needed, they fall into a pattern of criticism and/or competition with rare overt displays of affirmation. Failing to give affirmation, they're unlikely to receive it.

Take a Moment . . .

to evaluate how often you verbally affirm your children. When was the last time you praised an achievement, admired a quality, expressed gratitude for their contributions to your well-being, or encouraged their pursuits? How often do you do these things?

What Do Your Children Need from You?

Again, the specific needs vary from one individual to another. Yet most adult children need three things from their parents: *freedom*, *friendship*, and *love*.

Freedom

Many people have a distorted idea of freedom. When we ask students what freedom means, the most common response is, "Being able to do what you want, when you want to do it." And frequently someone will add: "as long as you don't hurt someone else."

This is an egocentric notion of freedom. We prefer to define freedom as the *opportunity to develop yourself and to relate meaningfully to other people*. In other words, when we say that your adult children need you to give them freedom, we mean that you need to treat them as adults. Allow them to grow as individuals and to establish meaningful relationships. Do so without your parental hand pushing them in the direction *you* think they should go.

You deny freedom to your children when you insist on being the micromanager of your children's lives. *Micromanagement* means you attend to every detail in accord with your predetermined goals and plans. In this case, your children's goals and plans are set by you rather than your children.

Peter, for example, a thirty-two-year-old man, wrote to an advice columnist for help. He'd never married and was successful in his career. When his aging parents needed help, he moved them into a home next to his. It seemed a reasonable solution to their needs. In a short time, however, the situation became "unbearable."

Peter reported that he had no privacy. His mother checked at night to see if his car was in the driveway. If it wasn't, she would call his friends and ask if they knew where he was. On his days off, his parents expected him to spend the time with them rather than his friends (after all, he didn't have any other family responsibilities).

In short, his parents limited his freedom. They didn't treat him as an adult. And, as usually happens, in trying to control his life and ensure his devotion, they alienated him.

Although it may be hard at first, you are capable of *choosing* to be flexible. Even when you don't approve of their plans, you can still be supportive. Monique shared this story:

> *My mom always assumed that I wouldn't leave home until I got married. This is what she'd done. So it was a shock to her when I announced that I was moving into my own apartment. I had finished college, was working, and wanted to be on my own. She couldn't understand this at first. But I have to give her credit. She not only agreed but even helped me hunt for an apartment. I know my move has been hard on her. She and my dad divorced years ago, and now she's alone. But we've become better friends since I moved out. We do something together at least once a week and don't bicker with each other the way we did when we lived together.*

Friendship

Freedom is the basis for developing *friendship*; your children need your friendship as much as you need theirs. And for the same reasons. Look again at the characteristics of close friendship that we listed earlier. They apply as much to your children as they do to you.

If you're not a friend, that is, if you continue to try to control your children's lives, your children will react in one of three ways: they will become or remain overly *dependent*; *rebellious* and *hostile*; or alienated and distant.

If instead you develop a friendship with your adult children, you'll have a relationship that's healthy for both of you. From your children's perspective, a friendship with you means such things as:

- You're there for them when they need you.

- You're enjoyable to be around.

- You're a good listener.

- They can feel good about themselves.

- They have no need to pretend to be someone they are not.

- They feel safe with you.

- You're supportive, not judgmental.

- You're affirming, but realistic.

- You respect their differences.

- You don't pressure them to conform to your ideals.

- You value their opinions.

- You're ready to receive and respect their opinion.

All of these are important components of a meaningful parent-child friendship. Hopefully, you began laying the groundwork for this friendship early in your child's life. If you did, the transition to adult friendship will be far smoother—the next step in an already vital relationship.

Love

Love? "That's a given," you say. "I have spent years protecting, providing for, and nurturing my children. Isn't that what love is all about?" You're correct, of course. An important part of love is what you do for your children. As adults, they still need for you to express your love through what you do: the warmth with which you greet them, the attention you give to their birthdays and other special events, the concern you show about their well-being, and so on.

However, what you say is also important. *Verbalize* your love. Tell your children how proud you are of them and how much you love them. And don't underestimate the importance of the direct statement: "I love you." A friend looked morose as he said to us: "Here I am, fifty years old, and I've never heard my dad say he loves me." He went on to acknowledge that he knew his father loved him, but he longed to hear the words.

Children never outgrow the need for parental love. It's your love that gives them a point of security and stability in a world that sometimes seems chaotic and unpredictable. It's your love that reminds them that they're of value. It's your love that buffers them from the full destructive impact of stressful life events. It's your love that imprints their beings with the warmth that they can carry with them throughout their lives.

Reflecting and Planning

Earlier you reflected on what you needed and what you thought your parents needed when you left your parents home. Now do the same for yourself and your children:

In your separate journal, list five or more things that you need from your adult children. You can start with general needs, but translate them into specific behaviors. For example, your need for continuing contact may take the specific forms: "I need to hear from or talk to my children at least once a week. I need to visit with my children at least twice a year."

List five or more things that you think your children need from you. Again, put them into the form of specific behaviors.

Tell your children you're reading a book about your stage of life and, as part of an assignment, have made a list of things you think they need from you. Share your list with them, and ask for their reactions. Then revise the list as needed.

For each item you've listed, devise a plan for implementing it with the input and approval of your children. For example, if you live in the same area as your children, you might have them to your house for dinner on a particular night each month. Or you might plan to have Sunday brunch with them on a regular basis.

Remember to get feedback from your children about any plans you devise. A mother who lives at a considerable distance from one of her sons told us that she decided to start sending him an email every other day:

> *I asked him first if it would be too much. He assured me it wasn't. I knew that was true when I was down with the flu one week and did little else but lie in bed. I talked to him on the phone at the end of my illness, and one of his first comments was that he really missed getting my email messages.*

His feedback let her know that her emails were as meaningful to him as they were to her. Thus, they continue to use this method to stay in regular contact. Attend to feedback from your children. You may continue, modify, or change your plans based upon what you hear. Keep in mind that active listening and flexibility are essentials for establishing a successful relationship with adult children.

5

Restructure Your Parenthood: Feelings, Behavior, and Communication

Adjusting the definitions of your needs as a parent, along with those of your children, is one aspect of restructuring your parenthood. The other parts of this undertaking entail you and your children learning how to relate *emotionally* as adults, *behave* as adults, and *communicate* as adults.

We say "learning" because few people make the transition to dealing with their children as adults naturally and flawlessly. Indeed, we've worked with some who never make the transition and continue to act as though they're the parental caretakers of immature children.

Relating Emotionally to Your Adult Children

The words may sound strange to you—learning to *relate emotionally* to your adult children. "My feelings," you may counter, "result from particular experiences I have with my children rather than the choices I make." To a large extent, this is true. For example, Joan, whose last child left home two years ago, told us that she gets really angry when her eldest son, a busy attorney, seems annoyed when she telephones his office. "I only call him," she says, "when something important happens. Since I don't abuse the privilege, I really get mad when he won't give me a few moments of his time. I don't *choose* to feel angry, it just happens." Joan makes a valid point. We don't choose our emotions, we just have them. They're neither good nor bad, they just are.

However, two things need to be said. First, while you can't control how you feel at a particular moment, you can control how you *behave*. Thus, when Joan gets angry with her son, she can choose to rant and rave, retreat into a hostile silence, become verbally abusive, or deny her anger and act pleasantly. Or she can have a reasoned discussion with her son about the basis for her anger. Remember, whatever the emotion, you're a mature adult and can act on your feelings in various ways.

Second, there are a number of emotional "tasks" that you need to complete in order to relate well with your adult children. In particular, you need to: experience forgiveness for parenting mistakes, resolve any lingering past hurts, and trust your children to survive their mistakes. Completing these tasks depends upon your recognition of the first point—that you can choose to act in various ways when you're experiencing a particular emotion. Your completing these emotional tasks also depends upon your awareness of the importance of emotions in the quality of relationships. Therefore, let's briefly examine the vital role that emotions play in relationships.

Emotions as Relational Tools

Emotions are powerful relational tools. You use your emotions, including your observation of the emotions of others, to gather and convey information as you relate to people. For instance, if you observe disgust in someone, you may assume that you've done or said something that the person finds offensive. You also use emotions to manipulate the behavior of others. Anger can intimidate. Cheerfulness can attract. Depression can distance.

Think about some of the following ways that parents use emotions to gather and convey information, as well as to manipulate their children's behavior both when they were young and now as adults:

- Watching for various moods in a child to determine whether he or she is happy and well-adjusted

- Looking for signs of warmth and affection as indicators that they're fulfilling their parental role well

- Expressing pleasure and pride to reward and reinforce a desired behavior in their children

- Showing disappointment when a child doesn't measure up to parental ideals in order to spur the child to greater effort

Of course, the latter example often backfires. A student with perfectionist parents told us she feels that she'll "never measure up" to her parents' expectations, so she doesn't even try anymore. The final blow came when she brought home a report card with all As, except for one B. Her father's only response was to ask what she did wrong in the class where she got the B.

Parents also use real or feigned sadness to control their child's behavior. "I feel so lonely when I don't hear from you," Julie, a single mother of two, said with a pained voice to her daughter. She wanted the girl, who was away at college, to phone more often.

Some parents even use emotional distance to punish a child. Researchers have found that emotional withdrawal is a common way for parents to discipline children. The child soon learns the message: *You won't love me unless I act in a way that pleases you.*

✒ *Take a Moment ...*

to recall the way in which your parents used various emotions to shape you when you were a child. To what extent have you acted in the same way with your own children? In what ways did you relate emotionally to your children that are different from the way your parents related to you? How many of your patterns of emotional relating would you like to continue with your children now that they are adults?

Forgiving Yourself for Parenting Mistakes

Virtually every parent we know can come up with an answer to this question: What mistakes did you make as a parent that continue to trouble you? Here are some common answers we have heard:

- I didn't spend enough time with my children when they were growing up.

- I would lose my temper and handle him roughly when he was only a baby.

- I should have insisted that they measure up to their academic potential.

- I made him feel guilty about spending time with his friends instead of with me.

- I wasn't strict enough about who she hung around with.

- I didn't compliment him enough.

- She was difficult from the beginning—I finally just gave up on disciplining her.

- I pushed him to be athletic like me, but I only made him feel inferior.

- I should have stuck it out in the marriage. She was hurt terribly by the divorce and by our inability to get along after the divorce.

- She felt caught in the middle.

Perhaps you would include some of the same things in your list of parenting mistakes. Most people identify a pattern rather than an isolated event as their primary failure as a parent. We all can recall isolated instances when we did or said something that we wish we hadn't. But what we usually regret are the things we did repeatedly that we now regard as mistakes.

Are those mistakes important now that your children have clearly survived them? Will dwelling on your mistakes make anything better now? The answers to these questions depend on how you and your children feel and behave in the present. Can you identify whether or not your mistakes continue to affect them adversely? Clara, a single mother, regrets being too demanding on her son emotionally. But she sees no lingering, adverse effects. "Richard is married, a father, and lives in another city because of his job. I talk to him two or three times a month and visit with him two or three times a year." Her son, in other words, is differentiated and well adjusted to his separate family life. He also has a loving relationship with his mother.

If you do see lingering adverse effects, you need to discuss the matter openly with your child and seek forgiveness for your mistakes. Seeking forgiveness begins by acknowledging to your child the way in which you believe you failed as a parent. You can then ask for forgiveness and a chance to repair your relationship.

Carlos, who had a brief career in minor league baseball, realized that he'd pushed his son unmercifully to excel in sports. "Looking back, I realize that I was determined to have another chance through José to make it in the big leagues." However, a sports career wasn't what José wanted. And Carlos' determination made José feel pressured and anxious. Eventually it caused a rift between father and son. "I was amazed at José's bitterness and anger, and it forced me to do some serious soul-searching," Carlos recalls. "It finally dawned on me what I had done to José, and I asked his forgiveness. Fortunately, he gave it to me and the anger between us is gone."

In contrast to Carlos, Clara mainly needed to forgive herself. She felt guilty. And you can't relate in a healthy, adult way with anyone if you're always trying to make up for past mistakes for which you feel guilty. Clara was overly sensitive about initiating visits with her son and his family lest it appear that she was still a demanding mother.

As Clara realized, it can be harder to forgive yourself than to forgive others, or to ask others for their forgiveness. Rationally, she knew that her son loved her. Emotionally, she still struggled with her guilt. She found release eventually through the following process of self-forgiveness—a process that can work for you as well.

- Remind yourself that all parents are flawed. Even if you could go back, erase the mistakes, and start over, you'd simply make a different set of mistakes.

- Remind yourself that love can neutralize the damage of parental mistakes. Clara's love nurtured her son well, in spite of her mistakes.

- Visualize forgiveness. Sit down in a quiet place, relax, close your eyes, and picture your child smiling at you, affirming his or her love, and telling you that you are forgiven.

- Visualize yourself—your body and your mind—being suffused with the healing warmth of forgiveness as you affirm that you forgive yourself.

- Focus on the joys of the present and future rather than the mistakes of the past. Whenever your thoughts revert to past mistakes, stop them.

- Tell yourself that you're forgiven and that you're now in a new and gratifying relationship with your children.

Repeat any part of this process as often as your relationship requires.

Resolving Past Hurts

Clara had another problem with her son that, for a time, impeded their relationship. In her effort to keep Richard emotionally close to her, she'd tried to dissuade him from going away to college. She argued that there were good schools in their area, and told him that if he insisted on going away she wouldn't help him financially. Although it was hard for him, he went anyway and managed on his own.

Richard appeared to deal well with other instances of his mother's emotional demands. But for a few years, he harbored the feeling that Clara had abandoned him at a time when he really needed her. Clara knew that he felt that she had really let him down. But neither of them talked about their feelings.

They could have continued their silent alienation indefinitely. This is what happens in some families. A hurtful incident is never resolved because no one is willing to address it, or at least one of the hurt parties refuses to discuss it. It's simply always there; an unhealed wound that drains the relationship.

As the parent, Clara finally decided to take the initiative. One day she asked Richard how he felt about the college incident. She assured him of her concern and desire to mend their relationship. Clara listened to Richard's account, and he listened to hers. They didn't agree on all the details entirely, but now they could hear each other's perspective. Each expressed their regret and agreed not to let it further harm their relationship.

If you need to settle any unresolved issues from the past that affect your relationships, the following steps can help.

- Acknowledge that the hurt exists and agree to discuss and come to terms with it.

- Listen to each other carefully, making sure that each of you is satisfied that the other understands your feelings and recollections.

- Accept each other's version of the incident and its effects as true, even if it doesn't agree with your version.

- Take additional steps, if needed, to heal the hurt.

- Forgive *each other*. Your task isn't to determine who was right and who was wrong (each of you contributed to the problem), but to understand and become reconciled.

- Discuss how you can move on and enjoy the kind of relationship you would each like to have.

When we suggest that you take additional steps, we mean, for example, one of you may want to repeat one of these steps. Or one of you may need some additional information, or reassurance that the other's regret over the hurt is genuine. Or if one of you senses that the other is still hurting, you may need to simply ask: "What can I do now to help ease your hurt?"

Trusting Your Children to Survive Their Mistakes

A third emotional task strengthening your emotional relationship involves learning to trust your adult children to survive their mistakes. You'll need to resist intervening when you're anxious or distressed about something that your child does or plans to do. Intervening may be appropriate if you see your child doing something that is destructive to him- or herself, or to his or her spouse or children. Even then, before you intervene you should run the situation by someone whose judgment you trust.

On the other hand, resist the impulse to intervene simply because your children are acting in a way that falls short of *your* ideals, preferences, or dreams for them. This includes such situations as the following:

- Your child pursues a career that you deem beneath his or her abilities.

- Your child seems too strict or too permissive with his or her children.

- Your child and his or her spouse are spending too much and saving too little.

- Your unmarried child stays up late and parties too much.

- Your unmarried child is getting too involved with someone that you believe isn't right for him or her.

- Your child neglects responsibilities—religious, social, or political—that you insisted the child fulfill when he or she lived in your home.

- Your unmarried child resists the notion of marriage, or your married child resists the idea of having children.

We could extend the list indefinitely. The point is, you will be bothered by some of the things your adult child says and does because they're contrary to what you think is the right way to talk and behave. Or they're contrary to what you think is best for your child. Indeed, you may be right. Some of your child's actions may turn out to be mistakes. Your child may regret them. But unless the situation is so serious that it's potentially destructive and necessitates possibly even outside intervention, you must learn to trust your child. He or she will survive those mistakes and learn from them— just as you did.

Behaving as Adults with Your Children

If your emotional relationship is in order, you're well on your way to *behaving* as adults with your children. In essence, behaving as adults with your children means that there's mutual responsibility for what happens. Let's think about the implications of *mutual responsibility* at first generally, and then specifically in terms of traditions and activities.

Mutual Responsibility

As we noted in the last section, your children have the right to make their own choices, to live with the consequences of those choices, and to learn from their mistakes. We've seen parents act as if they were still responsible for insuring their adult children's safety and well-being. Moreover, we've seen adult children, particularly when their parents are aging, reverse roles and begin to parent their parents—insisting on what their parents should and should not do (even when the parents are quite capable of making their own decisions).

By definition, mutual responsibility means that you and your adult children treat each other as responsible adults. If you impose your opinion about something that your child is doing, and he or she then tells you not to interfere, you must accept the rebuke graciously. You may even need to apologize. The request came from a responsible adult. In turn, if your child interferes inappropriately in your life, you must be open about your disapproval and remind your child that you're still a responsible adult.

This may not be easy. When family is involved, the friendship metaphor doesn't always fit precisely. For example, if you have a good friend who's alienated from her brother, you might do nothing more than agree with your friend that her alienation is understandable. But if you have a son and daughter who are alienated from each other, the situation is more difficult to handle.

Marsha, a mother of two adult children, came to us with just such a problem:

> *My son and daughter hardly have anything to do with each other. It just tears me up. They only live a hundred miles apart, but if we didn't have them at our house for holidays, I don't think they would ever see or talk to each other. And it all started over a silly incident when my son-in-law said something that my son found insulting. They never liked each other anyway, but after this occasion they just settled into a cold war. What can I do?*

We asked Marsha if her children knew how she felt. She said they did. We asked if they had entreated her to mediate and bring about a reconciliation. She admitted that they had not. We told her there was little more she could do, then, other than to treat them equally and lovingly in order to show that she did not take sides or assign blame.

Parents can help alleviate sibling rivalry or jealousy when their children are young. But the children are responsible for finding a resolution if the problems continue into adulthood. They may be acting in a way that is detrimental to them (depriving themselves of the benefits of good sibling relationships), but it's still their problem.

"But it makes the family gatherings tense for everyone," Marsha reminded us. "So it isn't just their problem. It's our problem, too." "Tense," we replied, "is different from destructive or intolerable." We suggested that a little tension may be bearable if it provides the opportunity to show the children that they each are loved and respected. If the tension is too high, then there are alternatives, such as entertaining the two families separately at different times. "In any case," we told Marsha, "it is not *your* responsibility to make things right when your children are adults and have made it clear that they don't want you to intervene."

Traditions

We sympathize with Marsha's desire to have her family together for family celebrations. Traditions, including the way holidays are observed, are important. Traditions should generate feelings of warmth and solidarity, not apprehension and weariness.

Mutual responsibility is a way to maintain the warmth and solidarity generated by observing traditions. Mutual responsibility means that you and your child are accountable for preserving an adult relationship. You are no longer solely responsible for planning, hosting, and implementing family traditions. For example, Francine, a mother of four, shares how mutual responsibility rescued a meaningful tradition that had degenerated into a time of harassment for her:

> *When the kids were little, we made Christmas very special. We had a spectacular meal on Christmas Eve. The kids helped plan the menu and, of course, I did the cooking. Then we went to church. On Christmas morning, after we opened our presents, I fixed a fancy breakfast. And in the evening, I prepared another big meal for the extended family, which included, at the very least, both sets of grandparents.*
>
> *For some insane reason, I continued the same practice after the kids were grown, married, and had kids of their own. I don't have as much energy as I used to. I was exhausted by Christmas Eve from decorating the house, buying and wrapping presents, and socializing with our closest friends. And still, I had three special meals to fix for our growing family.*
>
> *I actually began to dread Christmas. Then two years ago as I was wearily thinking about all I had to do, I blurted out that it would be fun, and a great help, to have one of the Christmas meals at someone else's house.*

Francine's daughter-in-law offered to prepare the Christmas Eve meal. This broke the pattern; no longer was Francine solely responsible. Now, the children and parents alternate responsibility for the meals so that no one is overwhelmed. Christmas is once again a time of warmth and solidarity for Francine.

Francine's experience shows the importance of strong communication skills in a mature relationship. It was important for Francine to tell her family about how overwhelmed she felt in maintaining the family's holiday traditions. When she opened up about her feelings, this gave them the opportunity to discuss the matter, examine their options, and find a way to share the load. Their experience reinforces the fact that communicating as adults is essential to behaving as adults. We will discuss communication more fully in the next section.

Take a Moment . . .

to think about your family traditions. In what ways can you ensure that they become a mutual responsibility rather than your sole responsibility. Perhaps your children are away at college. Can they help with meals when they come home? Perhaps you have married children who can host the family celebrations at their home sometimes. Whatever the tradition—holiday observances, birthday celebrations, vacations, traditional family activities—think of ways to share the responsibility with your adult children.

Activities

People engage in all sorts of enjoyable activities with their adult children, from shopping to golf to picnics to dining out. Once again, such activities should be a mutual responsibility. This includes who initiates, plans, and pays for the activity.

Like traditions, shared activities generate warmth and solidarity. They can even be healing for troubled relationships if you engage in them as you would with a friend. Vincent, a lawyer, had a strained relationship with his daughter, Lucy, who was away at college. He had spent little time with her when she was growing up because of his heavy involvement in his work. By the time she was a young adult, Vincent was managing his workload better. He desperately wanted to repair the relationship. He let Lucy know that he would be in her town for a day and wanted to spend some time with her:

> *I'm sure Lucy thought I was coming there on business.*
> *But I had no reason to go other than to be with her. When*
> *we met, I could tell by the look on her face that she didn't*
> *quite know what she was going to do with me for the next*
> *few hours. So I asked her to show me around the campus.*
> *She began by hurrying me through the library and*
> *administration building. I knew she felt that I would be*

rushing off soon. I'd always done things hurriedly with her when she was little. So I deliberately paused a number of times and asked questions. Then I asked her where there was a nice place we could have lunch. We had a leisurely meal while I inquired about her classes, her friends, and her dreams for the future. And I told her about some of my dreams for her and some of the things she did as a little girl that I remembered fondly.

The longer we talked, the more she relaxed. My visit didn't solve everything, but it was the beginning of a new relationship with my daughter.

Vincent took on the responsibility of instigating an activity with his daughter that would be interesting for the both of them. It turned out to be a positive bonding experience that led to future shared activities. You, like Vincent, can incite your adult children to engage in such activities that bring you together.

Communicating as Adults

Parents generally reserve baby talk for their infants. When the children are no longer infants, the parents don't use baby talk any longer. Nor do they speak to their adolescents in the same way they do to their young children. Neither should you talk to your adult children as though they were adolescents.

Think of it this way. You and your children are *not* talking as adults when you:

- Attempt to exercise veto power over their decisions

- Instruct rather than listen

- Insist that your ideas are superior to theirs

- Refuse to discuss certain topics

- Declare what is correct rather than discuss an issue

- Make your children uncomfortable when they disagree with you

Some of these were appropriate when your children were young, but they aren't appropriate for adult children.

At times, your adult children may solicit your advice. More often, they want to discuss something with you or want your approval rather than your advice. They want the assurance that you'll continue to love them whatever decision they make. Or they simply want to share what they're doing with someone they love and respect.

In general, assume that when you talk with your adult children they aren't looking for advice, solutions, or guidance. Unless they explicitly ask for such things, assume that they want to talk with you as an *adult friend*. What does this involve? For the most part, communicating as adult friends includes *mutual sharing, listening,* and *enjoyment*.

Friends Engage in Mutual Sharing

Think about your conversations with a friend. If it is a true friendship, your conversation is a dialogue not a monologue. It's a sharing of feelings, ideas, fears, hopes, aspirations, your thoughts on latest political scandal, or the weather report. Thus, you talk together about everything from the profound to the mundane.

However, you probably didn't talk much about such matters with your children when they were young. Perhaps you shielded them from your own fears while encouraging them to talk about theirs. Perhaps you never thought they were interested in your aspirations, but you asked them about theirs. And you probably didn't say much about the weather unless it affected some kind of family activity.

But they are adults now. If you haven't already done so, it's time to start sharing those things that are important to you. Vincent told us that a major event that caused him to mend the relationship with his daughter was the death of his mother:

> *My mother was an enigma to me. She never opened up and talked about what was bothering her. Or how she felt about life or death or what was going on in the world. She never even really talked about what gave her pleasure. When she died, I realized that I was doing the same thing with my daughter. And I didn't want my daughter to one day say that I was an enigma to her.*

Friends Listen

The old adage that children should be seen and not heard reflects the idea that children are expected to receive information and guidance rather than to express opinions. The adage is wrong. Even young children need someone to listen and respect their viewpoint. We have on more than one occasion observed a young child physically grasp an inattentive parent's face so that the parent is forced to look at the child. It's a way of saying, "Please give me your attention and listen to what I have to say."

When children become adults, they still need their parents to listen to them—perhaps the need is even greater. They need you to listen to their struggles, hopes, joys, and their perplexities so that you understand the kind of people they are and want to become. With your children, as with anyone else, you listen effectively when you:

- Resist interrupting with rebuttals or criticisms

- Focus on what your child is saying

- Make sure you understand by asking clarifying questions

- Rephrase or summarize what your child has said

- Provide nonverbal signals of active listening—eye contact and nods of interest

- Maintain a nonjudgmental expression on your face

- Resist changing the subject until your child is clearly finished talking about the topic at hand

In these ways, you let your child know that you want to understand and support his or her feelings, thoughts, and dreams rather than criticize or judge them.

Friends Enjoy Their Time Together

Not all conversations between friends are serious. In fact, one of the nice things about friendships is the banter and the playfulness in conversations. We've found that having our adult children (and children-in-law) linger in conversation around the dining room table long after the meal is over is one of the great pleasures of life. Our conversations range widely. Sometimes the topics are light and frivolous—a funny person we've met, the latest books we've read, or a recent movie we've seen. Other times they are weightier—a nagging worry, an imminent decision, or a difficult relationship. But even when the topic is a serious one, we enjoy being with one another and sharing our concerns. This is a mark of adult friendship.

Reflecting and Planning

As you reflect on the way you relate emotionally, behave, and communicate with your adult children, what would you like to change? Which areas need to be strengthened? Focus on changing one area at a time. Use the suggestions and information given in this chapter to develop a plan of action.

Some of the necessary changes may be difficult or painful. If, for instance, you've never shared your fears or times of distress with your children, you may find it difficult to start doing so. But keep in mind, as Vincent said, that you don't want to be an enigma to your children. This doesn't mean you have to share everything. However, they need to know you as a real person with the full range of human emotions.

Other changes may be painless and even a matter to laugh about in the future. As a father told us:

> *My wife and I always paid for the meals when we ate out with our children, even after they were grownup. When our son married, we continued to pick up the check for him and our daughter-in-law. But my wife and I decided that we weren't treating them as adults. The next time we went out together, I took the check as usual. But I looked at our son and told him what his share of the bill was. I could see he was startled. But he paid. And from then on, we shared the cost. He laughs about it now as the time when he realized that we really saw him as an adult.*

6

Expand the Self

Arthur was a remarkable man. He was in his sixties when we first met him. He had no formal education beyond high school. He worked at a public utilities plant for thirty-seven years before he was forced into early retirement because of downsizing. This occurred shortly after his wife died and his last child left home. Arthur was alone and unemployed—circumstances that would have been the undoing of many people.

But Arthur didn't capitulate to adverse circumstances. He set out to rebuild his life. He lived on a large tract of land on the outskirts of San Francisco, California. He loved working outside, so he began a soon-to-be-successful landscaping venture. Three years later, once his business was well established, Arthur studied real estate and got his license as a broker. He then had two thriving jobs.

However, Arthur's new life was about more than work. When his son took a job with an American corporation in Brazil, he invited Arthur to visit. In preparation for his visit, Arthur enrolled in a language school and learned conversational Portuguese. The trip was a great success—the first of many for Arthur. In addition to his work and travels, he also was one of the most active volunteers in his community.

Arthur was in his nineties when he died. During the years we knew him, he was generally cheerful and thoroughly engaged with living. For us, he illustrates well how you can meet the challenge of expanding the self and living a full life when the nest is empty.

Take Stock—Assessing the Quality of Your Life

As you contemplate your own empty nest, *take stock* of your life. In particular, reflect on your *past* in order to appreciate what your life has been so far. Think about the *present* in order to evaluate where you are now. And think about the *future* in terms of what you hope for in the years ahead.

Take a Moment ...

to reflect on what you consider your achievements in life so far. What would you include on your list of accomplishments? What has given you a sense of pride? What would you like your children and your friends to remember about your life so far? Your answers may include anything—such as learning to control your temper, having successfully raised your children, professional achievements, or acts of kindness toward strangers.

Appreciating the Past

Note that we asked you to think about those things in your past that make you feel good. If you ruminate on past failures and mistakes, you will not have the energy and motivation necessary for launching yourself fully into the adventure of personal growth.

Evaluating the Present

On a scale of one to ten, where one means you're completely dissatisfied and ten means you're completely satisfied, rate those areas of your life right now that are central to your well-being. In particular, rate your:

- Emotional health _____
- Physical health _____
- Spiritual growth _____

- Intellectual growth _____
- Involvement with hobbies and leisure activities _____
- Work _____
- Intimate relationship _____
- Opportunities for adventurous and/or exciting things _____

Thinking about the Future

By rating each of the items in the previous list on a scale of one to ten, you've focused on the crucial areas in your life. Based on the scores, you may want to maintain certain areas as they are, while with others you may want to set some new directions. Cynthia and Walter, for instance, retired from their jobs shortly after their youngest child left home. Cynthia says they did some mutual soul-searching and, in the process, identified areas in which they needed new direction. As a couple, they rated their intimate relationships with friends a one. Cynthia rated her intellectual growth a five, while Walt rated his involvement with hobbies and leisure a four. These were areas where the scores were low so they decided to address these issues:

> *For years, we have been so wrapped up with our work and our children, that we haven't made many friends. Our social life beyond the family is almost nonexistent. Of course, Walt and I have friends from work, but we have no real close friends that we share. Now that the kids have scattered, we feel the need for friendship with other couples.*
>
> *I also plan to go back to college and take some courses. I went to work early on to help support the family and always felt deprived because I hadn't finished my degree. Walt has a number of things he wants to do but hasn't ever had the time for—like woodworking and gardening. At first, we wondered what we were going to do with ourselves. Now we wonder when we'll find the time to do all we want with our lives.*

Aim for Substance and Adventure in Your Life

A word of caution. Don't simply concentrate on trying to stay *busy*. Stories like those of Arthur and Walter and Cynthia can be misleading. You don't expand the self merely by staying busy. The point is to make the rest of your life an *adventure in growth* and do those things that you find *fulfilling*. Arthur was a man who loved the feel of the soil and felt thrilled at the sight of his growing vegetables. Cynthia is a woman who craves intellectual stimulation. Walter finds working with his hands to create something extremely gratifying.

You may, in contrast, prefer to expand the self by focusing inward. Maybe you've spent years in a noisy, busy household, and want to devote time to reading and meditation. Ron, an electrical engineer, told us that he received excellent training in his professional field but scarcely any time studying subjects outside of his scientific field: "I had minimal exposure to literature and philosophy in college," he said, "so I'm using this time in my life to catch up. I have a list of one hundred great classics of literature and am slowly making my way through them. I feel like a whole new world has opened up to me. I'm ecstatic!"

There are diverse ways to expand the self. Before getting involved with or continuing activities, ask a number of questions about them such as:

- Does this activity resonate with who I want to be?

- Does this activity provide personal gratification?

- Does this activity contribute to my self-esteem?

- Does this activity give me new insights into myself?

- Does this activity develop a skill?

- Does this activity increase my knowledge, or exercise my creative potential?

For an activity to be an adventure in growth, you should be able to give an affirmative answer to most of these questions.

Take a Moment . . .

to picture the7 kind of person you want to become. In particular, think about yourself five to ten years from now. In the areas you rated earlier—emotional health, physical health, spiritual growth, and so on—where would you like to see yourself? What new skills and/or achievements would you like to have? Write your thoughts down and keep your self-portrait in mind as we go on to think about your present and future identity.

Your Identity: Today and Tomorrow

"Who am I?" is a question faced by most empty-nesters. The answer is not only found in the past but also in the future. That is, the question must be addressed in conjunction with another: *"Who shall I become?"* What kind of person do you want to be? What qualities do you want to develop? What realms of life do you want to explore? Such questions are at the heart of any effort to expand the self. When you expand the self, you change your identity to some extent. Let's look, therefore, at the meaning of identity, and how it changes as the self grows.

What Is Identity?

When you answer the question, "Who am I?" you're describing your identity, that is to say, your understanding of the kind of person you are. Social psychologists have researched the answer to this question by having people write down as many responses as they can think of in a few minutes' time. The kinds of things that go into forming identity include factors such as the following:

- Your roles

- Your understanding of your personality and your abilities

- Your moral and spiritual commitments

- Your interpersonal skills

Your identity, then, includes all your roles (for example, "I am a woman, a mother, a daughter, a veterinarian, a precinct captain in local politics"). It includes the kind of personal qualities you see in yourself ("I am loving, spiritual, intelligent, attractive, sensitive, liberal, family-oriented rather than work-oriented, outgoing, and fairly traditional"). Finally, your identity may include some qualities that you define as undesirable ("I am hot-headed, clumsy, overweight, and stubborn").

How Do You Develop an Identity?

Your identity is shaped by a combination of factors: your genetic predisposition to certain ways of behaving; your work or career; your intimate relationships (parents, other family members, friends, and people you admire); your education; and your interactions with others within your various roles (how people such as teachers, co-workers, and extended family members relate to you and regard you).

Because your identity is tied up with experiences, it will change over time. Someone close to you (such as a parent or friend) might express deep gratitude for what you've meant to him or her, thereby enhancing some part of your identity. Someone new may come into your life and express admiration for skills that you never recognized in yourself, thereby adding a new dimension to your identity. Or you may embark upon some new venture that makes you more aware of your creative potential.

In essence, the business of living involves so many diverse and new experiences that your identity is in process, not in storage. Think about it this way. Reconstruct the person you were twenty years ago. In many ways, you're still that person—there's always some continuity in our identities. But if the you of twenty years ago could confront the you of today, wouldn't the old you find someone who is interesting, more knowledgeable, and who has skills, qualities, and achievements that the old you would have liked to have had? Wouldn't you disagree, perhaps even argue, about some things? Wouldn't you, in sum, give somewhat different answers to the question, *Who am I?*

Why Is Your Identity Important?

Your identity is an integral part of your well-being. You will be emotionally and physically healthier to the extent that you perceive your identity in positive terms. For example, you'll be healthier if you see yourself as:

- A successful spouse and parent

- A generally competent person

- An attractive and stimulating person

- Above average in certain things

- Actively pursuing personal growth

- Contributing to the well-being of others

There is a second reason why identity is important: people strive to act in ways that are congruent with their identities. If you think of yourself as a caring person, you'll strive to be caring (thereby strengthening your identity and honing your caring skills). If you think of yourself as a growing person, you'll be more open to new ideas and experiences (thereby facilitating your continued growth).

In other words, a positive identity is the foundation for the continued expansion of the self. As you recognize and affirm the positive aspects of your identity, you are at the same time opening the door to personal growth.

Another word of caution. You shouldn't ignore the negative parts of your identity, or try to convince yourself that you can do anything you choose to do. You need to recognize your deficiencies and limitations as well as your positive attributes. As Sarah, a housewife five years into the empty-nest stage, put it:

For the first time in my life, I think I know what I can say "yes" to and what I must say "no" to. And for the first time in my life, I feel comfortable saying both yes and no. A woman called and asked me if I would volunteer to go door-to-door in my neighborhood and ask for gifts to a charity. I'm a contributor myself. But I know I'm not good at asking other people to give. So I turned her down. I can and do help the charity. But asking people to support it by going door-to-door isn't a way in which I feel I can help.

Sarah realized that being aware of her limitations keeps her from wasting time and energy on matters that are counterproductive to personal growth. Being aware of your deficiencies enables you to identify some specific ways you need to grow. And being aware of your positive attributes gives you resources and guidelines for this growth.

Programming Your Personal Growth

Much of life is already programmed for you. Your parents, school, work, and children consume a considerable amount of your time and energy. Now that your nest is empty you have the opportunity to *program* a greater chunk of your life. Sarah finds this exhilarating:

I don't feel as hounded by all I have to do. Not that I have all kinds of time on my hands. But there's a big difference between being pressured by what you have to do and by what you want to do. And knowing that I have so much more time to do what I want to do is fantastic!

Sarah has also discovered that what she wants to do includes things (such as spending an afternoon reading or walking for an hour in a nearby park) she probably would have considered a waste of time at an earlier period in her life.

There are two mistakes that you want to avoid. One is to *mindlessly program* yourself to keep busy. As we noted earlier, your aim should be an adventure in growth, not merely staying busy. The second mistake is to *avoid* programming—to drift with the currents of life and give little or no thought to your future identity.

Programming means that you're taking charge of your life and setting your sights on personal growth. You are content neither to be pushed along wherever the forces of people and circumstances direct nor to be consumed by meaningless responsibilities and activities. Rather, you're going to embark upon a journey of discovery and growth. There are four tasks in the journey:

- Setting goals

- Nurturing the underdeveloped aspects of yourself

- Exploring new interests and ventures

- Practicing the sacrament of the present moment

Let's consider each of these tasks.

Set Goals

When you set goals, you avoid to a large extent the mistakes we have noted: drifting aimlessly or drowning in busyness. As you set goals, keep in mind your present and future identities—who you are and who you want to become. In other words, your goals should reflect both your capabilities and your potential.

Furthermore, you should set both short- and long-term goals. Even if you've reached the emptynest stage at a relatively later age, do not neglect the long-term goals. We heard a wise psychiatrist advise a friend who was retiring: "Create long-term plans for your life. Otherwise, you're telling yourself to die."

Write out your goals in your separate journal. This will help you to remember them and make certain that they're consistent with each other. In addition, it will help you to evaluate them in terms of a number of other important characteristics; namely, whether they are specific, realistic, and relevant.

Making Your Goals Specific

When we ask people to formulate goals, they often stop with goals that are too general, such as, "I want to become a more exciting person." That's a good beginning. But what does it mean to become a more exciting person? Goals are meant to give you directions for action, and you can't act on goals that are too general or too vague.

We suggest that you begin with such general goals but then quickly make those goals more specific. Here are some specific actions that might help you to meet the general goal "to become a more exciting person":

- Take a class in oil painting

- Learn to play tennis

- Go on a weekend meditation retreat

- Get a mud bath

- Travel to Austria

- Read all the novels of Dickens

- Plant a rose garden

- Hike the Grand Canyon

- Coach a Little League team

- Renew your friendship with a local couple of your college friends

- Go deep-sea fishing

- Take up quilting

Note that each of the above is specific enough to enable you to make concrete plans for implementing it.

Incidentally, you shouldn't consider your list of goals to be "done." Periodically, you need to review and modify them. For example, ask yourself are you so engrossed in oil painting that you're no longer concerned about caring for your rose garden? Is a rose garden not something you want after all? Do you have new interests that you'd like to add to your list? Like your identity, goals are in process, not in storage.

Making Your Goals Realistic

In reaction to his empty nest, Peter declared that he had set the goal of retiring at age fifty and spending the rest of his life traveling. He found traveling very exciting and fulfilling. He stated that his goal was to visit every country in the world. He was determined to work doubly hard for the next seven years to accomplish this goal.

However, it wasn't a realistic goal. For one thing, although he was in a lucrative profession, Peter's income depended on the state of the economy as well as his efforts. Second, the work schedule he set for himself endangered his physical and emotional health. Third, he overlooked the fact that his wife was not as convinced about leaving her career as he was about leaving his. Finally, the political situation in some nations limits accessibility for tourists.

Goals can be unrealistic for various reasons. The man who said that one of his goals was to visit Austria could afford to do so. Some people can't. The woman who said she wanted to take up oil painting has artistic skills. Some people do not (although you should base such a judgment on evidence and not merely on the fact that you've never tried). If your goals are beyond your financial or other means (like our friend Peter who wanted to visit *every* country), they're probably unrealistic.

However, this doesn't mean that your goals must be easily attainable. You'll want to challenge yourself at times. Recall that one of Arthur's goals was to learn conversational Portuguese. This wasn't an easy thing for a man in his seventies. There were times when he despaired. Still, he persisted and was able to use the language when he visited Brazil.

Making Your Goals Relevant

Remember, you're setting goals right now in order to help you meet the difficulties of facing the empty nest. This is a long-term situation, so your goals should be relevant to your overall goal of personal growth. It's okay, for instance, to have a goal of organizing your garage or redoing the room your child has vacated or finally visiting your aunt Maggie. But if these are simply tasks that you believe need to be done but do not contribute to the expansion of your self, you need different goals—goals that *will* contribute to your personal growth.

So review your list and assess each of the goals in terms of how it will contribute to your personal growth. An easy way to do this is to ask the same questions about your goals that we suggested you ask about your activities in the "Aim for Substance and Adventure in Your Life" section earlier in this chapter.

Nurturing the Underdeveloped Aspects of Yourself

One of the tasks you face in the middle years of life is to *nurture those aspects* of yourself that are *underdeveloped*. Taking the time out to develop certain aspects that have been neglected will help to strengthen your sense of identity as well. An empty nest gives you more time and opportunities to do this. There are three steps to the task:

- Cultivate the qualities you desire.

- Nurture your dormant interests and skills.

- Affirm and develop your opposite-sex qualities.

Cultivating desired qualities demands that you address your deficiencies. For instance, if you've always been short-tempered, you may want to cultivate patience. If you generally cave into the demands and wishes of others, you may want to cultivate assertiveness. If you've been too dependent on the opinions of others for your feelings of self-worth, you may want to cultivate self-esteem. If you've been troubled by jealousy, you may want to cultivate the ability to trust. And so on.

Cultivating such things as patience and the ability to trust will be more or less difficult for you depending in part on how long you have practiced the opposite qualities. You may find that a spouse and/or friends can help you. Talk over your goals with them and discuss together how you can cultivate the qualities you desire. Self-help books can also be useful. If the quality you want is still elusive, a therapist can help.

Nurturing dormant interests and skills involves attending to those things that you have not had time to pursue or develop fully. You still won't have time to attend to all of them, so select whatever you feel most passionate about. A professional woman tells how she made the selection:

> *I enjoy art, and I've done some oil painting. My friends*
> *expected me to pursue it avidly now that the children are*
> *grown up. But I frankly don't have the time to pursue*
> *everything I'm interested in as long as I'm working. I decided*
> *to take on one new venture. I love to sing, but I've never*

sung in public. So I joined a chorus that performs for people in retirement homes.

Finally, affirming and developing your opposite-sex qualities involves aligning yourself with the natural process of maturing. As people age, they tend to take on more of the opposite-sex qualities. Men tend to become more nurturing and women tend to become achievement oriented as they grow older.

Some people resist these tendencies. They get stuck in the gender roles they accepted during the child-rearing years. They believe that such roles are the "natural" or at least the most appropriate ones for men and women. But achievement-oriented men and nurturing women are societal ideals created to sustain an arrangement in which men are breadwinners and women are mothers and homemakers. There is no reason why both men and women should not be both achievement oriented and nurturing.

To nurture your opposite-sex qualities, then, is not to betray your past. It is not to abandon your manhood or your womanhood. It is, rather, to take on the complementary qualities of the opposite sex so that you become a more complete person.

Exploring New Interests and Ventures

In setting your goals, consider *new interests* and *ventures*. Again, Arthur was a good example of someone who took the empty nest as an opportunity to pursue new ventures. Recall that he started a landscaping business. You expand the self when you pursue those things that you have dabbled in but never fully explored. Test out your talents by taking on some totally new projects. The question is not merely "What am I interested in?" but "What *could* I be interested in?"

Here are a few examples of interests that people have tried to do that they never even thought about before the empty nest years:

- Studying astronomy
- Jogging
- Learning Arabic
- Taking piano lessons
- Cross-country skiing
- Bird-watching
- Practicing hatha yoga

• Reupholstering furniture

The previous list is only a sampling, of course. If you want to get a better sense of the full range of interests and ventures available, go to your local library. Start at the beginning of the nonfiction stacks and scan the topics. You'll probably find more things that pique your interest than you could possibly pursue in a lifetime. Or look through your local community college catalogs. Sometimes just reading the class descriptions can spark interests you never knew you had.

As you open yourself up to new ventures, you may even encounter an opportunity that involves a major change in your life. Sheila and Tom are a professional couple whose willingness to embark on a new venture took them to a place they never expected to go:

> We both had lived in the Midwest for most of our lives. It was our home, the place where we raised our children. Five years ago, our oldest child took a job in another city and our youngest went away to college. Our nest was empty, but life was good. But then Tom and I both received an offer from a firm in California. One thing you have to understand is that we had never even been to California. And like many of the people we knew, we believed that it was a place filled with strange people who couldn't fit in with normal society.
>
> We struggled with the decision. The offer was really a good one. If our children had still lived at home, we would never have considered it. But we finally decided that we might never have such an opportunity again. We were determined to live out our lives with the idea that there's always a new adventure awaiting us. We took a short trip to California and actually fell in love with the diversity and excitement. So we accepted the offer and moved. And it's been one of the most rewarding moves of our life.

Tom and Sheila assert that they have grown enormously since their move. In Sheila's words: "The challenge of a new area, the intellectual stimulation, and the new experiences have enriched our lives and our marriage."

Practicing the Sacrament of the Present Moment

"When I was twenty-five," an empty-nest woman reported, "I spent most of my time wishing for something different. I was always thinking about what was ahead. Now I try to focus on and enjoy each day." We understand her perspective. We used to belong to a futurist organization and avidly read the futurist literature. One day a thought struck us: we are so focused on the future that we are missing out on the joys of the present.

Of course, you need to attend to the future. This is the point of setting goals. But you also need to practice the *sacrament* of the *present moment*. That is, you need to be fully engaged with what is happening and what you're experiencing at the moment.

A few years ago, we did research on people's experience of joy. We collected more than a thousand experiences and analyzed them to identify the sources of joy in people's lives. We also looked at ways in which people can increase the number of joyous experiences in their lives. Among other things, we found that being fully engaged with the present moment—letting experiences really penetrate you—opens the way to greater joy.

For example, a woman told us about being at a concert, getting caught up in the music of Mozart, resisting her typical practice of observing those around her, and experiencing unalloyed joy. And a father told us about the joy he experienced when he resisted his tendency to think about his work and became fully engaged in reading a bedtime story to his daughter. Such experiences expand the self. They connect you more closely with your world. They give you new insights. They enhance the quality of your relationships.

From time to time, you may need to remind yourself to focus on the present moment and let an experience penetrate your being. Make it a practice to clear your mind and take note of what you see, hear, smell, and feel. Practice the sacrament of the present moment and you will discover an intriguing way to expand the self.

Reflecting and Planning

At the top of a blank sheet of paper, write: "Who am I?" Give yourself three to five minutes to write as many answers as you can. Use these answers—along with what you wrote about the kind of person you want to become—as a guide for programming your personal growth.

You may already have some ideas about how you want to expand the self, but go through the exercise of reflecting on your present and future identity and then setting some goals anyway. This is important for two reasons. First, unless you lay out the full range of possibilities, you might shortchange yourself by choosing the first thing that comes to mind. An empty-nester said that he had anticipated turning his son's room into an office and beginning a long-cherished dream of writing a book. He dabbled with the idea and even made some preparations. Then he took time to think about all the possibilities, and decided to focus instead on his spiritual growth by reading, meditating, and attending retreats.

The second reason for examining all the possibilities is that you might begin a new venture and then decide that it isn't what you want after all. A woman set out to read the complete works of Shakespeare. She found a set of the works at a used bookstore. After a few weeks of struggling through two of the historical plays, she gave up. She was not enjoying her goal. "Now what do I do with myself?" she asked. In laying out all the possibilities, she found a number of answers to the question. And if the next thing she tries doesn't work out, she now has contingency plans.

As you write down your goals, put some in as many as possible of the areas of life we identified earlier, such as your emotional, physical, or spiritual state of being or your intellectual pursuits, hobbies, and intimate relationships. Whatever you choose to focus on, remember to take this time as an opportunity for doing things you find adventurous and/or exciting.

7

Reach Out

A colleague shared the following story with us:

As a young man, I struggled for several years with some severe personal problems. One day I was feeling near the end of my rope when an old man stopped me on a street corner. He was bent over and walking with difficulty. He asked me to help him cross the street. I was so preoccupied with my troubles that I found even such a small request just one more burden. But I took his arm and led him across the street.

When we got to the other side, he smiled at me and asked me if I felt better. The question startled me. I thought about it a moment and told him that yes, I did feel a little better. He went on to explain that when he looked at me, he knew I was very troubled. "I'm not as helpless as I look," the old man said with a chuckle. "But I told myself that here was a young man who needed to help someone who was even worse off than he was. So don't worry, my friend. God will take care of both of us."

I just stood there and watched him walk down the street. And as I did, I realized I was thinking about someone other than myself for the first time in weeks. And it felt good!

Although his problems didn't instantaneously disappear, our colleague says that the experience helped him recognize the value of reaching out and helping others.

You Need to Reach Out

In his 1879 novel, *The Egoist*, George Meredith described the self-focused life of Sir Willoughby Patterne whose chief goal in life was to protect himself from any person or situation that might prove distressing to him. At one point, Sir Willoughby, the quintessential egoist, says: "As far as I can, I surround myself with healthy people specially to guard myself from having my feelings wrung; and excepting Miss Dale [whom he wanted to marry] I am not aware of a case that threatens to torment me (Meredith 1968: 123)." Such a self-absorbed life is devoid of those human connections that enrich an individual.

The Lure of Self-Absorption

Of course, it's impossible to be totally self-focused and an effective parent at the same time. However, now that your children are raised and have left home, you may face a subtle lure to become more self-focused. Having devoted two or more decades to rearing your children, you might think "Now it's my turn." In a sense, it is. Yet your turn doesn't need to degenerate into self-absorption.

In chapter 6, we encouraged you to take stock and assess who you are and what you want to become now that you're an empty-nester. Seek new adventures, expand your horizons, and program a personal journey of discovery and growth. But be careful here. Although these tasks focus on personal growth, they don't exclude *reaching out* and contributing to others. In fact, reaching out to others is an important element in expanding the self and personal growth.

Three Traps to Avoid

There are three common, but erroneous, beliefs that can impede efforts at reaching out:

1. When you reach out to others, you're taking time and energy away from expanding the self.

2. Unless your motives are completely altruistic, your efforts aren't *really* worth much.

3. If you don't feel like it, don't do it.

Let's briefly examine each of these ideas.

When you reach out to others, you are taking time and energy away from expanding the self. Expanding the self and reaching out do not represent an either/or choice. You don't have to choose between them. On the contrary, expanding the self and reaching out are intertwined—each is an integral part of fashioning a new dimension of life.

Every time you reach out, you expand your self. Moreover, every time you expand your self, you are better prepared to reach out. For example:

- As you develop new interests, you become a more interesting person and are able to relate to a wider range of people; and as you relate to a wider range of people, you'll develop new interests.

- As you hone your interpersonal skills, you'll be more helpful to others; and as you help others, you'll further improve your interpersonal skills.

- As you nurture your spiritual self, you'll be better prepared to help others with their personal struggles; and as you strive to help others who are struggling, you'll find yourself growing spiritually.

Hopefully, you're convinced. You'll be expanding your self at the same time you're reaching out to others. In fact, you may find an opportunity to do both where you least expect it. But you might question: "How does my trip to Costa Rica, that I've always dreamed about and am finally taking, influence my ability to reach out?" The answer is, it may or may not *directly* affect your reaching out, but it can have an *indirect* impact. Indirectly, the trip to Costa Rica may heighten your appreciation for other cultures, broaden your perspectives, and add a dose of zest to your personality (which will be enjoyable for others). As a result, you are more engaged with life and more open to new experiences. Thus, you are more likely to effectively reach out to others.

However, a trip can also affect your actions more directly. You might, for instance, have an experience that prods you to be helpful to others. Here is Ben's (a recent empty-nester's) experience:

My wife and I were driving in the French-speaking part of Switzerland and came to a barrier in the road. Neither of us speak French so we didn't know what the sign on the barrier said. But we realized that we would be unable to travel to our destination by this road. Unfortunately, we didn't know any other road to take. So we stopped at a service station where I asked the attendant for help. Much to my frustration, he didn't speak English. I asked help from another customer, but he didn't speak English either. But when I showed him on the map where we wanted to go, he nodded and indicated that I should follow him.

As we followed the man's lead, we realized how grateful we felt to have found someone who was going to the same place we were headed, and who knew an alternate route to get there. After about ten miles, he pulled over to the side and motioned that we should continue on this same road. Then, in my rearview mirror, I saw him make a U-turn and go back the way we had just come.

We were astonished. He wasn't going where we were going at all. But in his kindness, he drove miles out of his way to help two lost strangers. His thoughtfulness has stayed with me and made me much more concerned about the strangers I encounter. I look for opportunities to help them the way that man helped us.

In expanding the self by taking a trip to Switzerland, Ben also had an experience that led him to reach out more to others.

Unless your motives are completely altruistic, your efforts aren't worth much. This idea is routinely expressed in our cynical culture. We often hear the media question people's motives, asking for example: Is a political leader acting in a particular way because he or she cares about the people or because of concerns about reelection? To be sure, people frequently act in seemingly helpful ways because of ulterior motives. They ingratiate themselves with another person in order to manipulate that person for personal gain. But motives—whether defined generally as good or bad—are seldom that simple.

There is a mixture of motives in most of what we do. And if part of the motivation for reaching out is to ease guilt, to feel good, to gain status, or to simply avoid saying "no" to a request, does that make the behavior worthless? Not at all. Someone will still be benefiting from your efforts.

Think about your parenting experiences. Were all of the positive things you did for your children driven by pure love? Did you ever do something you would have preferred not to do, but you still tried to look interested and act as if you were enjoying yourself? Did you ever urge a child to continue with an activity—such as music lessons, sports, or Scouts—because their participation personally gratified you in some way?

The point is, what you did for your child was motivated by a mixture of such things as love, concern, responsibility, guilt, selfish interest, and personal desires. One or more motive may have been predominant in any particular situation, but it's unlikely that you ever acted purely from a *single* motive—whether it was a good one or a bad one.

Similarly, various motives will undoubtedly drive your efforts at reaching out. But look at it this way. A hungry person who receives food from you or a hurting person who receives support from you will find the help no less important because you acted in part to avoid feeling guilty. People in need aren't concerned about the purity of your motives, only about the availability of your help.

If you don't feel like it, don't do it. We have mainly heard consumers of pop psychology voice this idea. They have read books that advise them to do such things as put themselves first, take control of their lives, and not allow anyone else to interfere with their pursuit of happiness. We believe that some of this advise is good. Some of it isn't. And often even the good advice is distorted into a determination to put personal desires and gratification before all else. This translates into such statements as: "I'm going to take care of me and let others take care of themselves," or "I'm going to do what I want to do and not what someone else wants me to do."

We'd like to share with you a personal experience that illustrates the fact that doing only what you "feel like" doing can lead to some missed opportunities for both reaching out and expanding the self. For about ten years, we led a marriage support group in our community. Our participation was voluntary. At the time, we were working full time as university professors with a full load of teaching, research, and publishing responsibilities. The group support met weekly on Wednesday nights. On many of these nights, we went with reluctance, longing for the ease and quiet of a night at home after a day of hard work. Occasionally, we came home frustrated and discouraged because of a low turnout or conflict that arose between some of the couples. A few times we considered disbanding the group.

However, we persisted with the venture in spite of the occasional negative feelings because we believed in the importance of helping people build solid and satisfying marriages. In the final assessment—based on feedback from couples who participated, on what we learned, and on relationships we established and still maintain—leading this group turned out to be a high point in our lives. If we had acted on the principle that "I only do what I feel like doing" the group would have been short-lived. By refusing to allow momentary feelings to dictate our behavior, we had a decade-long experience that has enriched us immeasurably and contributed something important to many other people.

Take a Moment ...

to estimate the amount of time you spend on various activities in an average week. How much time do you give to such things as work, family relationships, household tasks, recreation and leisure activities, self-development, and reaching out? Do you need to reallocate your time? Could you give some more time to reaching out? As an interesting exercise, keep a time journal for a week or two to see how accurate your estimates are.

The Rewards of Reaching Out

We have already suggested that reaching out is inherently rewarding. Let's look at some of those rewards: enhanced physical and emotional health, better interpersonal relationships, and the building of your community.

Reaching Out Enhances Your Health

People who do volunteer work for nonprofit organizations such as the Red Cross, the Peace Corps, local hospitals, the League of Women Voters, Big Brothers, or children's literacy programs often experience what is called a *helper's high*. Like the runner's high, the helper's high gives the individual a unique experience of well-being.

Research has shown that the health benefits of reaching out are not fleeting, however. Among other things, reaching out has been associated with:

- Increased energy

- Feeling good about yourself

- Good overall health, including less pain and fewer colds

- A sense of emotional well-being

- Increased ability to deal with chronic diseases

- Increased ability to handle stress

Some people say they have pleasurable physical sensations while they are helping others. They feel physical warmth and increased energy or strength in their bodies. Others are more aware of the emotional benefits—a feeling of peace, an increased sense of self-worth, and even a lifting of spirits if they've been feeling low or depressed.

Reaching out will not cure all of your physical and emotional ailments. At the same time, many who do reach out find that it makes a significant difference. Here are two accounts of how reaching out alleviated emotional turmoil. The first is from Olivia, a single mother:

> *When my daughter went away to college, I found myself really struggling with feelings of loneliness and depression. But the worst time came when she spent Thanksgiving break with her father. Not only had I not seen her for months, but I had to spend the holiday alone. It seemed an unbearable situation to me. I decided that I would never spend such a miserable Thanksgiving again.*
>
> *But what could I do? It occurred to me that there must be other people in my same situation. In fact, I realized that there are people in worse situations. People who don't have homes, for example. So the next holiday my daughter spent with her father, I volunteered to help cook meals for homeless people. I still missed my daughter, but I found that I could cope with her not being there. Actually, I more than coped. I felt a real sense of accomplishment. I enjoyed myself so much that I've been thinking about asking my daughter to go with me the next time we spend a holiday together.*

And Ruth, another empty-nester, shared this story with us:

> *Three years ago, my son, Donald, dropped out of school because he got hooked on drugs. I have never felt more devastated in my life. After he came home, I insisted that he get treatment and he refused. So he left and wouldn't come back home. For a while, I thought I would go out of my mind. I alternated between rage and depression and anxiety. I felt like I was on the edge of a breakdown when a friend told me about a program she'd volunteered for at our local public library. It was a program helping kids for whom English is*

*not their first language with their homework. She said they
needed more help and asked if I would volunteer.*

*At the time, I couldn't imagine doing it. I told her about
my problem with Donald and about how upset I was. She
urged me to give it a try anyway. "It might serve as a healing
experience for you," she said. So I agreed. "I can always save
my breakdown for when school lets out for the summer," I
told her. And I wasn't being funny.*

*After working with the kids for a couple of weeks, I felt
better and stronger. I realized that helping them was keeping
me together. Fortunately, before the start of summer vacation
my son returned home and agreed to get help. But I decided
to continue working with those kids. It's one of the best things
that's ever happened to me.*

We could give you other examples, but clearly reaching out is of
great value not merely to the recipients of help but to the helper as
well.

Reaching Out and Improving Your Interpersonal Relationships

As you reach out, you'll find your relationships with people
generally improving. There are a number of reasons for this:

- Reaching out makes you feel better about yourself. And the
  better you feel about yourself, the better you relate to others.

- Reaching out fosters a certain calmness and emotional well-
  being that makes you a more attractive person.

- Reaching out increases your understanding of human struggles and human behavior.

- Reaching out allows you to view situations in terms of how
  you can genuinely assist others.

- Reaching out shows people that you are interested in them
  for their sake rather than purely for your own.

Simone, a woman who frequently lectures to business groups,
impressed us with her story. She reminds herself before each lecture
to think about the people in the audience. In particular, she reminds
herself that they are there to learn something useful, not to be
impressed with her knowledge. She also tells herself that the people
in her audience are struggling with various problems and challenges.

And this has made a difference in the way the audience responds. Simone has noticed that people appreciate and respond positively as they realize that she is interested in them also.

> *When I used to focus on impressing people with my knowledge and ability to communicate, I would get compliments. I thought I had succeeded. But when I started focusing on trying to share with people something that would help them, I got very different responses. People would come up and share their struggles with me and tell me how much I had helped them. They greeted me warmly and seemed to bond with me. I certainly didn't get this kind of response when I was mainly trying to impress them.*

Reaching Out Builds Community

Reaching out helps build a sense of community—a sense that you're part of a group of people united by various bonds. This happens for a number of reasons:

- It is contagious. As you reach out to others, you also encourage them to reach out.

- It creates good feelings both within those who reach out and those who are helped. When you feel good about life, you're more likely to feel linked with those about you.

- Reaching out is a sign of concern for others. Perceiving that you belong to a group of people who care about each other greatly enhances the sense of community.

- Reaching out creates new ties with people. You get to know both those you help and your co-helpers.

An empty-nest mother had an experience in Africa that illustrates the way in which reaching out can be contagious:

> *While on a safari in Kenya, my husband and I decided to visit some villages to experience how people really live. One evening we arrived by bus in an out-of-the-way village and couldn't find a hotel. As we trudged down the road with our luggage, an African man drove up, stopped his car, and asked us what we were doing. We told him we were trying to get to know African people by visiting some of their villages and were looking for sleeping accommodations.*
>
> *He put us up for the night at the missionary settlement where he worked. He gave us supper, then showed us how to*

use the mosquito netting while we slept. We offered to pay him for his efforts, and he simply said he would see us in the morning. The next day, we again offered to pay him. We'll never forget his reply: "One day you will also have an opportunity to do something for someone, just as I have had the opportunity to help you. Do it. There is no payment required."

It was an awesome moment. Ever since, we have watched for opportunities to help strangers. You never know how much influence you will have. We've recently received a letter from a teenaged runaway we had met outside a fast-food restaurant. He was obviously hungry and in need of assistance. He eagerly accepted our offer to buy him a meal.

While he ate, he told us his story. When he had finished, we gave him some money and insisted that he call his parents and let them know that he was okay. We also gave him our address and telephone number in case he needed further help. In his letter, he thanked us for feeding him and talking to him and helping him get in touch with his family. He was back home now and had returned to school. He said he would never forget the way we had helped him and promised to help others whenever he had an opportunity.

How to Reach Out

Hopefully, you're convinced of your need to reach out. Hopefully, you're also convinced of the *rewards* of reaching out. Now what? What, exactly, does it mean to reach out to others? How do you go about it? Where do you start?

Reach Out to Your Social Network

You can start with the people around you. There are always people in your *social network*—family, friends, co-workers, acquaintances, neighbors—who need some kind of help and to whom you can reach out. In particular, you can offer your *presence* or your concerned *ear*.

Offer your presence. There are many people who are lonely. The best gift you can give to them is your company. Perhaps a relative who is confined to home or a neighbor who lives alone could use your friendship. Clark and his wife live in an urban apartment complex. He found a way to reach out:

There are a number of elderly people in my complex who are confined to their apartments most of the time. I discovered them by talking to neighbors and the mailman. So I introduced myself to several of them, told them that I lived nearby, and wondered if they would like an occasional visit. To my surprise, every single one of them was delighted at my offer.

I began stopping by their apartments a couple of times a month. I don't stay long. Maybe a half hour or so. Sometimes my wife comes along. We talk about whatever they want. One man is very interested in politics. I don't agree with his views, but I let him tell me all about what's wrong with our politicians anyway. One of the women loves to relate the latest escapades of her grandchildren. Sometimes we just talk about the neighborhood.

Occasionally, I bring them cookies or cupcakes that my wife has baked. And sometimes one of them will give me something. The woman who likes to talk about her family gave me a handkerchief she had embroidered with my initials. I was quite touched by it. It's amazing how much each of them appreciates my visits.

Offer your ear: listen. Offering your ear may seem to be a small thing. However, it isn't trivial. Nor is it easy. It isn't trivial because there are many people who desperately need to have someone listen to them. It isn't easy because most of us have never really learned to listen. Our minds wander, we interrupt before the other person has finished, or we respond to what we *think* the person has said rather than what he or she has actually said.

We frequently teach a training class for caregivers. An important part of that class is learning to listen. To be an effective listener requires you to:

- Focus on what the other person is saying. The objective is to keep your mind from wandering and to attend to both the verbal and nonverbal cues that are necessary to understand what the person is saying.

- Refrain from jumping in with a quick solution when someone is talking about a problem.

- Be accepting of the other person even if you don't agree with his or her position.

- Resist formulating a response in your mind before the person has finished; instead, try to summarize in your mind what the other person is saying so that you remain focused on him or her.

- Ask questions only when necessary to clarify for yourself what the other person is saying or feeling.

- Repeat back what you've heard so that both you and the other person know that you have understood.

We have received gratifying feedback from those who have taken our classes. A single mother who took the class both to expand herself and to reach out after her last child left home told us the following incident:

I'm the kind of person who always tries to solve everyone's problems. I think I developed the habit partly because that's the nature of the work I do—finding solutions for customers who are dissatisfied. About a week after our session on listening, a colleague of mine asked if she could talk to me. We agreed to meet at lunch and walk through the park.

As we walked, she told me about a problem she was having with her husband. In the past, I would have quickly interrupted her and suggested a number of things she could do. But I kept the training in mind, bit my tongue, and tried to focus on what she was saying.

She talked for forty-five minutes. We never got to lunch. But as we walked back to work, she hugged me and told me how much I had helped her. Helped her! Can you beat that? All I did was listen and show her that I understood and that I cared. I never did get around to any solutions.

The point is, of course, that many times people are not looking for solutions. They're looking for someone who will listen to them so that they can fashion their own responses or solutions, or just so they can share their burden with someone else. Another woman, a teacher, who took the class shared this experience:

I'm accustomed to talking. However, when you gave the session on listening, I vowed I would try to be a better listener. Since then, I've resisted quickly chiming in with an opinion in this class and made a real effort to listen to what others are saying. It hasn't been easy, but I think I'm making progress.

I belong to a bridge club, and last week one of the other members asked to talk to me about a problem. I practiced my new skills. I listened. And when she was finished, she said to me, "Millie, you're the only person I know who has listened to my problems. Talking to you has meant more to me than you'll ever know. I'm really grateful that you're my friend."

Listening is neither trivial nor easy. But it's an important skill to possess, and using it is a wonderful way to reach out.

Take a Moment ...

to reflect on your listening skills. Do others approach you as someone who will listen? How well do you follow the rules of effective listening? If you want to hone your listening skills, work with your spouse, another family member, or friend who is also interested in becoming a better listener. Practice by assigning one of you the speaker role and the other the listener role. Then reverse the roles. Discuss together whether each of you followed the rules of effective listening. Then go over ways you can improve your skills.

Where appropriate, offer other kinds of help. Be realistic. There are people who will take advantage of your desire to reach out. They will want to borrow large sums of money, ask you to do time-consuming tasks for them, or make other inappropriate demands. Use good judgment when offering other kinds of help. Reaching out should be a response to needs, not a support for irresponsibility or dependency.

In other words, effective reaching out is not a knee-jerk reaction to every request but a measured response in terms of both what is appropriate and reasonable. Your reaching out might include such things as spending a few hours caring for a relative or friend with Alzheimer's disease so that the caregiver's spouse can get away for an afternoon. Or taking care of a friend's pet while he or she is on vacation, or volunteering as an aide at your local elementary school. The possibilities are endless and the needs are everywhere.

Reach Out Wherever You Happen to Be

Once we attended a lecture where the speaker asked people to look around them at the audience and then raise their hand if they were sitting near someone who looked like he or she was struggling with a problem. Only a few people raised their hands. We think that this was because, when you look at people, individually or in a group, they often look trouble-free. Indeed, when you ask someone, "How are you?" the answer typically is "Fine."

However, the world is filled with people who are hurting or struggling or in some kind of need. Think of your own life. How often can you truthfully say that you have no pain, no worries, no challenges, and no struggles? If your answer is that you're rarely troubled by such things, you're either unique or oblivious to reality.

Reach out to others as you go about your daily activities. You don't know who will benefit from your small acts of kindness. But you can be certain that your actions will lighten people's loads, create good feelings, and help build community. Consider a few examples of acts of kindness that people have shared with us:

I bought a couple of items at a greeting card store in the shopping mall. The clerk miscalculated the total amount, and I pointed it out to her. At one time, I might have been irritated because of the extra time it took to correct the error. But I smiled as I showed her the mistake to let her know that we all make them and I didn't think it was intentional. She sighed and said, "Thank you for not getting angry. I've had two customers in here already today who got very upset with me for no reason. One claimed that I should have waited on her first, and the other was a man who snapped at me when I asked if I could help him, and told me not to be so pushy. I really appreciate your understanding."

I was standing near a woman waiting for the elevator. She dropped a pen she'd been holding, and I quickly reached down and picked it up for her. "Thank you," she said, "I have a bad back and that really helps me."

We were on vacation and wanted to hike in this park. But it was a maze of trails and we were afraid we might get lost. As we debated what to do, a cyclist came by and asked if we needed help. We told him about our concerns, and he asked if we had a map. We said no. "Here," he said. "Take mine. I can get another one." He rode away and we set off on a great day of hiking. And once again we were grateful that people can be kind to strangers.

Helping Out Organizations

Helping is most meaningful when you have person-to-person contact. Yet a lot of helping can only be done through organizations that need your support. CARE is an organization that gives assistance to people throughout the world who are impoverished. You probably can't travel around the world providing assistance directly, but you can provide financial support to the organization. The Red Cross helps people who are victimized by natural disasters. You may not be able to help those people directly, but you can support the Red Cross efforts through your donations. The Salvation Army has a variety of programs that help the down-and-out. You may not be able to help such people directly, but the Salvation Army couldn't continue without your financial support. And there are hundreds of similar organizations who can't survive without your assistance.

In addition to financial assistance, of course, help organizations need your physical support. Every community has an array of help organizations who depend on volunteers. For example, here is a sampling of organizations in our community that are looking for volunteers:

- Hospitals that need gift shop clerks, receptionists, and waiting room hosts and hostesses

- Hospices that want people who can do respite care, run errands, or participate in bereavement support

- Organizations looking for people to be trained in and serve as negotiators in conflict situations

- Agencies looking for volunteers to tutor and read to children, or to teach English as a second language

- A prisoner outreach agency that needs people to volunteer to make a one-hour visit to a prisoner each month

- Museums that can use guides, clerks, and handymen

- Art galleries looking for someone to greet visitors and answer questions

- Thrift stores that need drivers to pick up donations, people with construction experience, and merchandise sorters and organizers

- Animal shelters that want volunteers willing to groom and exercise animals

- Science centers that need people to explain and demonstrate exhibits or serve as receptionists or clerks

- Government agencies looking for volunteers to act as mentors, tutors, and role models for youth who are at risk for getting involved with gangs

- Schools that need people to help with various physical education activities before, during, and after school

- Youth organizations that want volunteers who can engage in mentoring, tutoring, fund-raising, and help with group and special projects

- Help organizations that are looking for people to pick fruit and produce donated by farmers and distribute the food to the needy

- Home-care services that want people who will assist elderly patients with grocery shopping, transportation, respite care, friendly visits, and special projects

This list represents only some of the opportunities for volunteer work. If you are interested in working through an organization, you should be able to secure a similar list of nonprofit organizations in your area that need volunteers. You are likely to be startled by the sheer number of opportunities you have to reach out through such organizations.

There are also numerous special interest groups for which you can volunteer. An empty-nest mother, for example, found working with a historic preservation group to be a fulfilling way to reach out in her community:

It's really exciting to get involved with a group of people who are enthusiastic about what they're doing. It gets my adrenaline going. We recently rescued a run-down but historic building from the hands of developers and helped refurbish it for community use. This makes me feel useful at the same time I'm having a lot of fun!

Other people have reached out even farther than their local communities. They have devoted all or a portion of their vacations to work with Habitat for Humanity building houses for the poor, or to work with the group founded by Mother Teresa caring for the dying. Some have joined the Peace Corps. Again, you may or may not be able to do such things. But whether in your neighborhood, your community, or another state or nation, the opportunities are both diverse and numerous.

Find Your Passion

We once heard a man complain that he tried to do some volunteer work but that it didn't make him feel any better. Unfortunately, this man had overlooked an important rule for reaching out: *find your passion*. As we have stressed before, the point isn't to merely consume your time. Your efforts won't pay off unless you find something or someone to whom you can give yourself with some degree of passion. Find a way to extend yourself to others that is both exciting and rewarding.

Finding your passion may be a trial-and-error procedure. You can't expect some kind of helping activity to be an endless thrill a minute, of course. But if you find yourself simply going through the motions and not feeling like you're doing something worthwhile and fulfilling, you need to reach out in a different way.

A good way to begin is to consider what interests you. For instance, would you like to do something involving children, the elderly, the homeless, the sick, or the poor? Or do your interests lie more in the area of politics or particular causes? It was only after she asked herself such questions that Jan found her passion:

> *While I was trying to deal with the gloom of my empty nest,*
> *a number of my friends advised me to get out and find*
> *something new to do. So I tried. I did some volunteer work.*
> *Nothing seemed to fill my emptiness. One day I asked myself*
> *what it is that I really enjoy. And the answer came*
> *quickly—children! I volunteered to help in a program for*
> *abused children. But even that wasn't quite working. I still*
> *yearned to parent. So I took in a foster child. That was what*
> *I needed. I'm now on my fifth child. And I don't think I'll*
> *ever stop.*

Jan's experience, incidentally, illustrates an important point. Once you identify an area that interests you, you may still have to engage in trial-and-error until you find the right organization or the right way for you to reach out.

Reflecting and Planning

As you think about reaching out, keep in mind that there may be some aspects of reaching out that will be drudge work. Reaching out is seldom, if ever, an experience of unrelenting joy. As Ben, the father of three adult children, put it:

> *My wife and I volunteered to run a respite program in our*
> *church. We have a lot of elderly members who are the chief*
> *caregivers for their ailing spouses. So we recruit other*

members to spend some time each week giving the caregivers a break from their responsibilities.

I must admit that I don't like some of the tasks we have. I don't like the paperwork or finding new volunteers when we need them. But overall it's been a very gratifying experience. I get a glow inside me when those elderly members tell me how much the program has meant to them.

We suggested earlier that one way to find your passion is to ask what broad areas interest you. It is also important to raise the question of what kind of skills you have or what kind of skills you would like to develop. You are unlikely to feel a passion for any activity for which you feel ill-equipped.

On a sheet of paper, make two lists. On one side write down broad areas of helping, including children, the aged, people with disabilities, health services, arts and culture, animals, adolescents, housing, literacy, charities, disaster relief, religious organizations, political groups, special causes (such as abortion, victims of abuse, and the environment), and any others that come to mind.

On the other list, write down your skills (including skills that you would like to develop). List your interpersonal skills (such as listening, caring, ability to establish rapport, ability to teach), organizational and administrative skills (e.g., filing, record keeping, scheduling, coordinating activities), and technical skills (word processing, use of computers, carpentry, sewing). Also list any particular talents or abilities you have (e.g., musical talent, artistic ability, facility with foreign languages).

Cross out anything in either of the two lists that you are sure you would *not* want to do or skills you would *not* want to use. You may know, for example, that you definitely would not want to work in the area of people with disabilities. You may know that even though you have strong technical skills, you would not want to volunteer to do word processing for any group.

Examine carefully what remains. Prioritize the areas that interest you. Note the kind of skills and/or abilities you could offer. Now set a date to look for an area in which you can reach out. Many communities have a central clearing house that can give you a list of all the agencies using volunteers. When you make contact with a particular organization, tell the person the kind of skills and abilities you have and would like to use in your volunteer work. You may not find your passion on the first try, but you will eventually. And you'll discover for yourself that reaching out and expanding the self nurture each other in the adventure of life.

8

Strengthen Your
Couplehood

This is a tale of two couples. In many ways their stories are similar. Both couples married in their twenties. Both believed that their union was forever and that their love was strong enough to endure any problems. Both were family oriented and wanted children. Both were devoted parents and enjoyed their children. Both reached the empty nest when they were in their early fifties. But that's where the similarities end.

The first couple, Joe and Alice, had their first child shortly before they celebrated their first wedding anniversary. In time, they had four children including a set of twins. When their children left home, they both felt a keen sense of loss. What to do? During the first quiet week in their empty house, they decided that they needed a change. Joe and Alice felt that new, different surroundings would give them a chance to take stock of their lives. And so they rented an isolated, oceanfront cottage and set off for a week together.

It was a disaster. By the third day, both Joe and Alice were ready to leave although neither admitted it to the other. By the end of the week, they were unable to hide their irritability and boredom. When they returned home, they frankly admitted to each other that they hadn't enjoyed being alone together. Unfortunately, their situation didn't improve over the next few months, and they began to consider the possibility of separation or even divorce.

The second couple, Phil and Maria, have two children. Like Joe and Alice, they struggled with a sense of loss when they found themselves in an empty nest. And they, too, decided to console themselves by taking a three-week trip together—the first one ever without a child along. They admit now that they were a bit apprehensive. They pondered such things as: Would it be as much fun without the kids? Would they feel lonely? They were in for a pleasant surprise. Phil describes the experience:

> *Not only did we not feel lonely, we had a ball! It was so relaxing because we could do just what we wanted. We didn't have to think about what the kids would like to do. We both love to visit historic homes and roam around in antique shops. And that's just what we did. Believe me, vacations have taken on a whole new meaning for us.*

Both couples have been devoted parents. But Phil and Maria also were devoted to their marriage while their children were growing up. As a result, the transition to the empty nest was relatively painless for them. They're now engaged in strengthening their marriage and finding it an exciting adventure.

Joe and Alice, in contrast, made two mistakes. The first mistake was to neglect their marital relationship for years while they concentrated on children and careers. They had grown apart without even being aware of it. The bond with their children made them oblivious to the slow erosion of their marital intimacy. The seaside vacation opened their eyes to the lack of vitality in their relationship. However, their second mistake was to assume that what they had in the early years of their marriage was irretrievable. If the empty nest stunned them into awareness, it also presented them with the opportunity to rebuild their relationship. Their error was in not seizing that opportunity.

If you arrive at the empty nest with a strong marriage, you have the chance to make it even better. If you arrive with a fragile marriage, you have the opportunity to rebuild it into a vital relationship.

✍ *Take a Moment ...*

to evaluate your marital satisfaction. Would you say you're entering the empty-nest stage of life with a strong and satisfying marriage, or with one that needs to be strengthened? Write down the reasons for the answer you give. Ask your spouse to do the same. Read through this chapter together, then compare your evaluations and work together on a plan of action for the future.

Marital Benefits

Marriage, of course, isn't an automatic boost to personal well-being. You don't have to look far to find people who can testify to the destructive consequences of a bad marriage. In fact, this is one reason to attend to your marital relationship—to avoid getting sucked into the morass of pain that characterizes a stressful intimate relationship. The other reason is to reap the benefits of a good marriage. Those benefits are numerous and important. Specifically, compared to people who have never married or are divorced, those who *are married* usually:

- Are physically healthier
- Are emotionally healthier
- Have lower rates of alcoholism
- Have lower rates of suicide
- Deal better with stress
- Have more satisfying sex lives
- Report higher levels of life satisfaction
- Are more likely to say they're "very happy"

Obviously, such benefits are only associated with those who have a *fundamentally* satisfying marriage. That is, you don't have to be satisfied every moment of every day about everything. Satisfying marriages are not conflict-free marriages. Even people with strong marriages occasionally think about their marriage breaking up—because of such thing as an attraction to someone else, weariness with a particular problem, or a momentary boredom with the relationship. But couples with a strong relationship work through the low times, enjoy the high times, and reap the benefits. Listen to what these individuals have to say:

I'm a champion of marriage. I've been married to Gino for over thirty years and love it. My husband seems to get better every year we're together.

When you ask me who I am, I don't even think I can answer the question without talking about my wife. I truly believe that she has helped me become a much better man than I would have been without her. Like most couples, we've had our difficult times. But my marriage is one of the best things that ever happened to me.

My husband is my best friend. I recently talked to a young woman who said that great sex is the most important thing in a relationship. I feel sorry for her if she really believes that. The most important thing is to be with someone you genuinely like as a person. Then everything else, including sex, falls into place. I would rather spend time with my husband than anyone else I know. I feel so fortunate that we're together.

The Marital Challenge

The potential benefits are great. But so are the hazards, as indicated by the increased divorce rate as people move into the empty-nest stage of life. Joe and Alice, whom we discussed at the beginning of this chapter, discovered this for themselves. As Joe put it:

I used to be surprised when a couple who'd been married for twenty to thirty years divorced. But when our last child left home, I understood why they did it. It isn't easy to be alone with one person when you've been surrounded by kids for most of your married life. We found that we had little to talk or laugh or dream about that didn't involve the children. And when we had an argument, the kids weren't there to distract us or cause us to pretend that everything was okay. We suddenly had to face each other and thrash it out on our own.

In other words, when the children leave home, your marital relationship is forced into prominence again. You face the challenge of a relationship that is partner-centered rather than child-centered. More particularly, you face the fourfold challenge of building and *maintaining satisfying roles, meaningful communication*, a satisfactory method of *handling your differences*, and a *vital physical intimacy*. We'll discuss ways to meet these challenges in the next section. First, let's look at the nature of each of these challenges.

Satisfying Roles

For many years, your roles of husband and wife have been maintained in the context of raising a family. With the children gone, you have the challenge of reworking your roles in a way that is mutually satisfying. Like Phil and Maria, you can give increasing time and attention to each other, bringing higher levels of vitality and fulfillment to your relationship. Or like Joe and Alice, you can withdraw from each other, allowing your marriage to drift along or even dissolve. Here are some questions to ask each other and discuss as you rework your roles:

- What do you think are the qualities of an ideal mate?
- Which of those qualities would you like me to develop more?
- How much should we do together?
- What kind of activities or interests would you like to pursue apart from me?
- How would you prefer to divide up the household responsibilities?
- What was going on during the best times of our marriage that we can recapture and do again?
- What can I do, or what can we do together, to enrich our relationship?

Meaningful Communication

Joe and Alice found it difficult to communicate with each other after the children left home. So much of their conversation had either included or revolved around the children that Joe and Alice were at a loss as to how to discuss anything else. The problem was compounded by the fact that they had become less compatible over the years. Outside of her children, Alice's primary interest was music. She attended concerts with her friends and was a volunteer usher at many events. Joe's major passion, however, was sports. He frequented as many football and baseball games as time and money allowed; otherwise, he was glued to the sports channel whenever he had a free moment.

On the other hand, Phil and Maria had a far different pattern of communication. From the earliest days of their marriage, they had made talking together a high priority in their marriage. Like Joe and Alice, the children had been a central topic of conversation for Phil and Maria. But they also talked about other things like work, politics, or books they were reading. And they made it a practice to reserve some time each day "to reconnect"—to tell the other what they were doing and feeling.

Not surprisingly, they were better equipped to handle what Phil calls the "deadly quiet" of the empty nest. This doesn't mean that they haven't faced tough challenges; rather it means that they were better prepared to handle them. In fact, developing and maintaining meaningful communication in their empty-nest home has produced some surprises:

> *After more than thirty years together, I find myself learning things about Phil that I never knew. He'll tell me something that happened in his childhood that I had never heard. Or he'll talk about something he's interested in that he's never mentioned before. And he says the same thing about me. It's wonderful, after so many years together, to discover new things about each other.*

In our study of long-term marriages, one of the characteristics of those in satisfying relationships was that their spouses were more interesting to them now than when they were first married. And one of the main reasons for this was that they had meaningful communication. You may or may not learn new things about your spouse when you establish meaningful communication. But you'll certainly find yourself in a relationship where you can openly talk about anything you wish. You'll be able to explore ideas, pursue fantasies, discuss problems, and probe each other's feelings. In essence, to have meaningful communication means that you're able to fulfill your needs to know and be known, to explore, and to share.

Handling Differences

What's the best way to deal with your differences? To resolve an argument? The way you handled conflict when your children were at home may not suffice any longer. While their children were at home, Joe and Alice dealt with their differences, for the most part, by denying or ignoring them. These efforts to deny or ignore, of course, translated into a silent, cold war. With their children gone, they could no longer hide their differences in the noisy background of their children's voices.

Phil and Maria also had to address the issue of how they handled their differences. Phil grew up in a family where arguments always ended up with someone shouting. Thus, he typically raised his voice when disciplining his children or arguing with his wife. Maria tolerated, though she was never comfortable with, Phil's style of arguing. A short time ago, Maria asked for a change:

> I don't ever remember my mother or father raising their voices when they argued. So this has been hard for me. Actually, Phil and I seldom have arguments now. But when we do, it only makes it worse if he raises his voice. It didn't bother me as much when the children were home as it does now. Maybe the noise level was so high in our home that raising his voice didn't seem that bad. Or maybe I've just gotten to the point where I need things to be calmer. But I don't want him to do it anymore, and I communicated this to him.

Phil and Maria are working on a mutually acceptable way to deal with their differences. It's important that you and your partner are satisfied with whatever method you use. If shouting at each other resolves issues to your mutual satisfaction, there's no need for you to change.

There is no single right way to deal with your differences. But there are some decidedly wrong ways. In thrashing out an issue, you should always avoid the following:

- Attacking your spouse's character or judgment

- Attributing motives to your spouse

- Saying things designed to hurt rather than heal

- Treating your opinion as the only right or moral position

- Refusing to listen and interrupting your spouse

- Thinking of the conflict as a competition in which one of you will win and one will lose

In sum, the challenge of handling your differences is to find a way so that:

- You are both comfortable with the process (which is different from saying that you enjoy the argument).

- You are both satisfied with the way issues are generally resolved.

- You feel good about yourselves, your partner, and your relationship once the issue is resolved.

Physical Intimacy

Physical intimacy includes sex. It also includes expressions of affection such as touching, hugging, cuddling, kissing, and holding hands. Do such things retain their importance after decades of marriage? Absolutely. We are creatures of touch. We need to touch and to be touched. Infants who aren't cuddled sufficiently can suffer physically and emotionally from the lack of touch. And touch is central to an infant's learning about the nature of its world.

Touch never loses its importance. In an experiment with library patrons, those who had been briefly touched by the librarian when checking out a book reported the experience in more positive terms than those who hadn't been touched. And this held true even for those who couldn't recall having been touched!

People often express their connection to and affection for each other by joining hands or hugging. Athletes celebrate each other with the high five. An embrace comforts the grieving. A handshake welcomes the stranger. In every culture, physical contact is a way of creating, building, and intensifying intimacy.

The challenge for empty-nesters is to be aware of the significance of physical intimacy and to enrich and foster it. In our research, 98 percent of those with happy, stable marriages say they kiss each other practically every day. Such physical expressions of affection are crucial to the maintenance of a meaningful sexual relationship. As one wife put it:

> My husband and I are very affectionate with each other. Lots of hugging, stroking, touching, and kissing. Sex just grows naturally out of that. I couldn't turn on sexually if the only time he touched me or kissed me was when he wanted to have sex.

Similarly, one empty-nest father observed:

> The older I get, the more I realize how important the expressions of affection are. Even more than the sex in the early days of our marriage, I remember laying in her arms at night. Her body was telling me she loved me and that I was all right. This kind of physical sharing was very important.

And it remains important for him. He gets a feeling of warmth and well-being when his wife puts her hand in his or cuddles up to him. You never outgrow your need for physical intimacy—both to receive it and to give it.

How to Nurture and Strengthen Your Marriage

When you *nurture* and *strengthen* your marriage, you're also expanding the self and reaching out. Recall that when we discussed expanding the self we included interpersonal relationships as an integral part of the task. You grow through your experiences with people. In a strong marriage, you each grow as you learn from and support each other. This means you're also reaching out to a particular other and enriching that person's life.

So what can you do to nurture and strengthen your marriage? How can you address the challenges we discussed earlier? Here are eight techniques that can help.

Confront Any Unresolved Baggage

Let's begin with an unappealing but necessary task. *Baggage* refers to hurts, disappointments, resentments, and differences from the past that remain unresolved. Facing up to them isn't an enjoyable task. But it's a necessary one if your marriage is to be a celebration of life rather than an endurance test.

One of the problems vexing Joe and Alice is that she can recall a number of incidents in previous years that still trouble her. They've never been resolved:

> *He still thinks it's funny that he took off and went to a convention in Hawaii and left me with the children. I could've gone with him. My mom offered to watch the kids. But no, he said we couldn't afford it even though the company paid his way. That's just one example of how he's always insensitive to my needs and feelings. He's been a great father. But he hasn't been very good as a husband.*

If Joe and Alice are to salvage and rebuild their relationship, they'll have to deal with lingering issues such as this one. The empty nest is a time to start fresh, to move ahead in your marital relationship unhindered by this kind of baggage.

Forgiveness is one of the most effective methods that we know of to deal with the baggage that strains so many relationships. It's a method that has typically been urged by religious leaders and is now advocated by many therapists. It works where there is seemingly no adequate solution. For example, Joe cannot revise the past. So what does Alice want him to do? It's a question she hasn't yet addressed. Ultimately, they may only be able to resolve the issue through forgiveness.

Forgiveness is not a simple or easy process. It isn't merely a matter of saying "I forgive you." To forgive means to forego any vengeance or retaliation and to let go of the hurt. It paves the way for reconciliation and renewal of the relationship. But in order for forgiveness to occur, a number of things must happen, including an opportunity to air grievances, accept responsibility, understand each other, and work together to make the forgiveness effective. This is how the process might work to resolve Alice's hurt and improve their relationship:

- Alice fully expresses her hurt and, through Joe's careful listening and feedback, is assured that Joe understands why and how much she has been hurt.

- Alice recognizes and acknowledges the way in which she contributed to Joe's hurtful behavior. This includes the fact that she asked her mother about taking care of the children before she talked to Joe about the possibility of her going on the trip, and that she was not open about her feelings when he said no to her joining him.

- Joe accepts the fact that Alice is hurt without making any judgment about whether her hurt is appropriate.

- Joe expresses regret over her hurt and the way in which it has troubled their relationship.

- Joe asks Alice to forgive him and to tell him how he can help her with that forgiveness.

- Alice asks him to avoid any such behavior in the future and says she'll let go of the hurt so they can begin to repair their relationship.

If, after a time, Alice finds herself still feeling the hurt, she needs to ask herself why she hasn't forgiven Joe. Does she still want to punish him? Is she reluctant to rebuild their relationship for some reason? Is there something more she would like for him to do?

Perhaps you don't have the kind of pent-up baggage in your relationship that Joe and Alice have. Many couples don't. But if you do, your first step in strengthening your marriage is to deal with it. You can't bypass this step and still go on to more enjoyable tasks.

Take a Moment . . .

to think about your marriage. Do you have any lingering baggage? Any past issues or incidents that are still bothersome to you and that detract from the quality of your relationship? If so, think carefully about how you can confront and resolve them. Is the problem some continuing behavior that needs to change? If so, how can you work together to change the behavior? Is the problem a past hurt that still troubles you? If so, what needs to happen for forgiveness to occur? If you have no baggage, be grateful and move on.

Become or Remain Best Friends

Maria summed it up well: "It's as important to like your husband as it is to love him. We enjoy each other's company. We spend a great deal of time together, and I'd rather be with Phil than anyone I know."

In the strongest marriages, spouses typically identify each other as their best friends. Being each other's best friends includes the following:

- You like the kind of person your partner is.

- You enjoy being together as much as or more than you enjoy being with anyone else.

- You look forward to doing things together.

- You confide in and support each other.

- You appreciate and affirm each other.

What can you do to strengthen the friendship aspect of your marital relationship? Begin by reviewing the preceding list and discussing together how you can work on each of the following items:

- How can you help each other develop or strengthen qualities that each of you admire?

- Which activities can you pursue that you both enjoy, and that allow you to spend more time together?

- What can you plan to do as a couple that you both will anticipate with enthusiasm?

- How can you help each other be open and accepting so that you can freely talk about your feelings, aspirations, troubles, and doubts?

- What can you do to remind yourselves to articulate your appreciation of each other?

Books, articles, and classes are available to help you with these various issues. There is a great deal, however, that you can do on your own. Brainstorm. Let your imagination go to work. Work together and turn the effort into not just a task but an adventure in your relational growth.

For example, consider the last point—how to remind yourselves to articulate your appreciation of each other. In many marriages, partners fall into a habit of silent appreciation. They value each other but don't verbalize their appreciation. This is unfortunate. We all need not only to be appreciated but to *hear* that we're appreciated. So perhaps you can come up with something equivalent to the string on your finger, such as a note, a picture, or anything that will remind you to articulate your appreciation regularly.

Begin an anniversary ritual of appreciation. Each year on your anniversary, sit down, hold hands, look at each other, and take turns verbalizing everything you admire, respect, and appreciate about the other. You'll find that the list will change over the years as you discover new traits to admire and appreciate in each other. You probably shouldn't limit your words of appreciation to your anniversary, however. Having a ritual simply can serve as a reminder. But go ahead and make them an everyday occurrence too.

Focusing on Romance

A substantial number of people who divorce in the empty-nest stage of life identify boredom as one factor in the breakup of their marriage. This means they weren't best friends. It also means the relationship was suffering from insufficient romance.

The question is: *How do you keep the romance in your marriage?* To a large extent, the answer is different for every couple. Yet there are a few things that we know enhance romance. For example, a Roper poll asked Americans what they considered the most romantic things to do. The five most frequently mentioned activities were:

- Weekend getaways

- Long-stemmed roses

- Candlelight dinners at a restaurant

- Bouquets of flowers (other than roses)

- Love letters

Please note that, with the possible exception of the weekend getaway, none of these items is necessarily expensive. For a small amount of time and money, you can add a great deal of romance to your marriage. Consider, for instance, a love letter. In our marriage enrichment weekends, one activity we typically include is having each person write a love letter to their spouse. We instruct the couples to write the letters separately and not to reveal any of the contents. We collect the letters and mail them. We have received enthusiastic feedback about this exercise. Everyone loves to receive mail—especially when it is a love letter from your spouse!

Many small things, then, can add romance to your relationship. They might include the unexpected love note, the unanticipated gift, the sincere verbal expression of appreciation, the thoughtful shouldering of a task when the partner is obviously tired, or the suggestion to try a new endeavor of some kind. In short, whatever you say or do that tells your spouse "I care about you, I'm thinking about you, and I want to share life's adventures with you" adds romance.

Take a Moment . . .

to write down five to ten things that you would define as romantic. Ask your spouse to do the same. Share your lists with each other. Each of you select one thing from the other's list and do it.

Having Regular Dates

Although you may have more time now that your nest is empty, you're probably not sitting around wondering how to fill your spare moments. If you're working outside the home, or if you're focusing on enhancing the self and reaching out, you may find yourself at least as busy as when the children were at home.

Regular dates are a way to maintain romance in your marriage. They're also a way to ensure that you take the time to strengthen your marriage in the midst of a busy life. Phil took an early retirement, hoping to enjoy a more leisurely pace of life. Instead, he found himself in a whirl of activity:

When you retire, people think you have lots of time. They feel free to call on you. Some of our relatives ask me to do things they never would've asked when I was working. Our local political club asked me to chair a committee. My university asked me to chair the local committee for alumni giving. I'm co-manager for a Little League team. I've also done a good deal of consulting work for several companies in the area. Plus friends frequently call and invite us to do something with them.

Both Maria and I felt like we weren't having enough time together. So we started reserving one night a week on our calendar as our date night. If someone asks one of us to do something on that night, we say we have prior commitments for the evening. This is our way of making sure that we keep the romance alive in our marriage.

Honing Your Communication Skills

Three problems in couple communication are common: lack of *self-disclosure* (particularly sharing one's feelings), *poor listening*, and *taboo topics*. Most people can learn to hone their skills with regard to each of these problems with some simple techniques and practice.

If self-disclosure is a problem, you can begin by reframing it. People hesitate to share feelings, for instance, because they believe that sharing makes them vulnerable to criticism or less self-sufficiency. Reframe self-disclosure by defining it as an essential road to both personal well-being and rich intimacy. Like many husbands, at age fifty-two Peter found it very difficult to start talking to his wife about his feelings. But with determined effort, he learned to do it and found it liberating:

The thing that startled me was that not only did my wife feel closer to me, but I felt closer to her. Many of my worries dissipated as I talked about them, and the rest were easier to handle once I shared them with her. I realize now that my wife is insightful and is able to offer me valuable advice. I've found that the more I open up to her, the better I feel about myself and about our marriage.

Remind yourself that self-disclosure is liberating, then practice it. If you find this difficult, try this exercise with your spouse. Both of you decide on a topic. Choose one that is nonthreatening at first. Then talk in turn, for three- to five-minute intervals, about whatever feelings the topic or incident creates in you. Continue with other topics or incidents until self-disclosure becomes more natural for you.

If poor listening is a problem, refer to the principles of effective listening we identified in chapter 7. Apply those principles in discussions with your spouse. You can hone listening skills by having the spouse who most needs to improve his or her skills apply the principles as the other partner speaks about a topic or incident.

Finally, there may be a few topics that you and your spouse decide are taboo—topics that you agree not to talk about. For example, you may have decided not to discuss politics or religion because you always wind up arguing and can't find any basis for agreement. We were talking recently with another couple when one of us mentioned a current political issue. There was a noticeable hesitation. Then the husband, Mike, said to us: "We don't talk about that because we've always violently disagreed." In their case, avoiding the subject worked well for them.

However, it doesn't work well if it's a topic or an issue that is essential to your life together. For example, many couples argue vehemently about money or sex. But it would be hazardous to their relationship to label these topics as taboo, avoiding them altogether. If you encounter this kind of issue in your relationship, try to resolve it by using the principles of communication and listening we have discussed. Also use the following principles for handling conflict. If the issue persists, you'll need the assistance of a counselor.

Developing Your Conflict-Resolution Skills

As we noted earlier, there's no single right way to settle your differences. But it's important that each of you agree upon whatever method you use. Couples with the most gratifying marriages try to adhere to the following principles:

- Take the point of view that "we have a problem" rather than "you are a problem."

- Attack the problem, not your spouse.

- Keep issues in perspective—nothing is more important than your relationship.

- Confront differences directly and soon—don't get stuck in a silent resentment.

- Remember that most issues are matters of differing styles or preferences—there is no right and wrong.

- Recognize that differences can be resolved in a variety of ways—come up with as many potential solutions as you can before pursuing one of them.

Some partners find the following technique useful when one or both of them feel that the other partner doesn't understand their position. It works this way: One spouse begins and fully explains his or her position while the other listens without interrupting—except for clarification. At intervals, the listening partner repeats the essence of what the other has said so that both are confident that the listener understands. Then they switch roles and repeat the process. Once they both have thoroughly listened and understood, they're then in a better position to find a resolution.

Exploring Your World Together

The empty nest provides an excellent opportunity for expanding your horizons and exploring your world together. *Exploring* doesn't just mean going on an expedition to an exotic island or an uninhabited region. You can also explore your own community. This is what Phil and Maria have started doing on their date nights. Maria searches the newspaper each week for events in their area and circles the ones that sound appealing. Phil is in charge of finding new and different restaurants. For example, they recently viewed an exhibit on Southeast Asian art at their local art museum and then had dinner at a nearby Thai restaurant. Maria reported that it was "a totally exotic evening."

Exploring your world, in other words, can profitably start in your own community. Once you've explored something, you may decide you don't want to do it again. "I discovered that I really detest going to hockey games," Maria said. But even those experiences will be a part of your shared history. You can look back on them with humor and with the pleasure of knowing that you experienced them together.

Celebrating Your Union

Think about your empty nest as a unique opportunity to *celebrate your marriage*. Instead of getting stuck in longing for your absent children, focus on the fact that the two of you have a second chance to be alone together. And think of every plan you make and every new adventure you undertake as a celebration of this new phase of your life together.

One empty-nester couple we know found a delightful way to celebrate. For their twenty-fifth anniversary, Willard suggested to his wife, Carole, that they identify twenty-five ways to celebrate their marriage during the coming year—one event for each year of marriage. They made up their list and put the events on their calendar. They did a variety of things, including taking a trip abroad, dining at a five-star restaurant, going with friends to a concert, painting their bedroom, trying out the beer at a local microbrewery, and spending a week of their vacation working with Habitat for Humanity. The point is, Willard and Carole made each event a celebration of their marriage. Painting their bedroom or spending a week working with Habitat was not an afterthought or something they did because there was nothing else going on. These adventures were a toast to their years together. How's that for imagination and romance?

Reflecting and Planning

We've discussed eight techniques for nurturing and strengthening your marriage. Working together, prioritize these techniques according to your own interests and needs as a couple. If you have any lingering baggage, of course, that should be at the top of your list. If in the unlikely case that you feel no need to enhance your skills or have no problems to resolve, you can move directly to the eighth point and plan ways to celebrate your marriage.

Once you have your list, decide how you want to proceed. A number of basic questions can be asked to help you get started, such as:

- What are we already doing well in this area?

- Have we done things in the past successfully that we could do again?

- What has to happen for each of us to feel improvement in this area?

- What specifically can we do individually or as a couple to bring about the improvement?

For instance, let's assume that the third technique—focusing on romance—is at the top of your list. What are you now doing that keeps romance in your marriage? What are some romantic highlights from your past? Could you repeat those behaviors or events? What would have to happen for each of you to feel more romance in your life together?

Each of you should then make a list of the kinds of things you find romantic. Be very specific and include behavior (such as, "When you come up behind me and kiss me on my neck," or "When you surprise me with a gift"), activities (such as, "When we go out to din-ner and really talk with each other" or "When we spend time at the beach"), and attitudes (such as, "You still find me sexy," or "You want to please me"). Your list can include things from the past as well the present. You might also get some additional ideas by asking some friends about their notions of romance.

When you have each developed a list, go over them together. You may eliminate some items (perhaps a European trip, for exam-ple, is out of the question financially, even though you did find it romantic) and you may have some additional ideas as you read each other's list.

Now take your revised lists and raise the last question: What specifically can each of you individually or as a couple do to enhance the romance in your relationship? Keep in mind that a lot of good ideas wither and die unless you make concrete plans to implement them. In other words, if you have specific activities that you both agree would add romance to your relationship, get out your calendar and set a date to do them. If they're individual behaviors, such as kissing the back of your spouse's neck, use some method to remind yourself to do it. And if you're the recipient of this expression of affection, let your spouse know how much you like it. An expression of pleasure is one of the best assurances that it will happen again.

9

Enlarging Your Social Network

We have lived all of our lives in large cities. Perhaps this is why we're so curious about small-town life. In fact, we often ask people who formerly lived in small towns or rural areas whether or not they would like to live there again. Amelia, a woman from a small Southern town, told us without any hesitation: "I sure would. I grew up in a town of a thousand people, and I had a thousand friends there. I could count on any one of them if I needed them."

Her response catches the essence of what we call a social network—that group of people you feel bonded to and can count on when you need them. You are a social creature and need other people in your life. But sometimes you need them for special reasons, such as providing support when your children leave home.

Max and Lily discovered this when they were struggling to come to terms with their empty nest. They each felt that much of their zest for life left along with their last child. After several weeks of solitary struggle, they finally turned to their social network for help. They needed others—to share their struggle and to provide words of sympathy, encouragement, and affirmation. So they invited several couples to a party launching their new phase of life. The gathering helped snap them out of the doldrums. With the aid of their social network, they were able to deal with their loss and embark on an exciting empty nest adventure.

Who Is in Your Social Network?

Most likely your spouse (if you're married), children, and relatives comprise an important part of your social network. However, we want to examine more closely two other vital components—friends and specific groups.

Personal Friends

You probably have both individual and couple friends in your social network. We'll discuss couple friends in the next section. Here we will focus on your personal friends. A personal friend is someone not related by blood whom you:

- Like as a person

- Enjoy spending time with

- Feel comfortable and relaxed around

- Share thoughts, feelings, cares, and hopes with

- Feel free to call on in time of need

Of course, some friends are closer to you than others. And you feel freer to call on a close friend in time of need than you do a more casual friend.

Personal friends are always important in your life. However, they take on added importance as you face an empty nest. They can provide the perspective, comfort, and companionship you'll need in adjusting to your situation. Listen to the experience of Sally, a single mother:

When my daughter left home, I had to deal with the loss by myself. I didn't have a husband around to help me grieve. I felt more alone than ever before in my life. And I keenly felt—and I still feel—the loss of family. Most of the time my work keeps me busy and satisfied. But unless my daughter comes home, weekends and holidays are depressing.

Sally desperately needs to cultivate friends. Friends help take up the slack in lost intimacy when the children are gone. And as Kelly, another mother, noted, they can do so even if you're married:

My friends became more important than ever when I hit the empty nest. Stu and I were both so preoccupied with our own feelings of loss when Holly left for college that we weren't much help to each other. So I turned to my best friends, Meryl and Paula, and they helped me make the adjustment.

   These friends are especially important to me because I miss my daughter and the companionship we had. I didn't realize how important female friendship was to me until my daughter left.

Couple Friends

In addition to personal friends, this may be a good time to expand your circle of couple friends. Singles sometimes find that having couple friends gives them a sense of being a part of a family. Married people find that spending time with other couples strengthens their own relationship.

Personal and couple friends may overlap. Kelly and her husband, Stu, are couple friends with Meryl and her husband:

Right now, Meryl is my closest friend. She and I have lunch at least once a week. And occasionally Stu and I go somewhere with Meryl and her husband, so I get an extra dose of her friendship.

   Stu understands my need for female companionship. He encourages me to spend time with Meryl and my other friends. And because he likes both Meryl and her husband, we have started doing more things together as couples. It's a plus that their kids are gone too. In fact, their's left before ours so they have an added perspective that really helped me. And talking about the kinds of things they're doing together has helped Stu and me realize how many opportunities we have now.

Groups

Whether you're single or married, and in addition to personal and couple friends, groups can be an important part of your social network. Thus, if you're struggling with a sense of loss, you might want to find a support group for empty-nest parents. Or start one on your own. If you want to expand your horizons and venture into something new (as discussed in chapters 6 and 7), you might want to find a group that pursues an activity that interests you. Or start one on your own.

Being a part of a group increases your pleasure with an activity. For example, you may decide to take up running in order to expand the self. You can do it alone. In fact, you may want to run alone to use the time for meditation and reflection. But you can also find a group that runs together regularly. And for many people, this intensifies the activity, and puts them in touch with potential new friends.

Or perhaps you're an avid reader and find that you now have more time to read. You might want to join a book group or start such a group. You'll gain new perspectives on what you read as well as increase your opportunity to make new friends.

How Your Social Network Enriches You

According to the song "People," popularized by Barbra Streisand, people who need people are the luckiest people in the world. In that case, we all must be very lucky because we all need other people. We all need a social network. Consider the following benefits.

Your Network Encourages and Supports Your Personal Growth

The clearest example is the support group. You may be striving to grow intellectually, emotionally, spiritually, or interpersonally. You may be struggling with some problem or habit. Whatever the aim of your personal growth, a support group can encourage and support your efforts. Sometimes it's the difference between success and failure. As a member of a weight-loss group told us:

> *I tried for years to lose weight on my own. I had gotten to the point where I was ashamed to go out in public and had little to do with anyone except my husband. And I was miserable. Then I joined a weight-loss group. At every weekly meeting we weigh in. We reward each other for losing pounds.*

If you haven't lost or if you've gained, you can just feel the disappointment in the air.

I've lost over 100 pounds. I feel like a new person. I'm getting out and meeting new friends. I've gotten a part-time job. My life is on a new track, but I don't think I could've done it without the group.

Personal and couple friends also support your growth. Lauren, an empty-nest mother who decided to quit a job she didn't like and venture out on her own, found her social network indispensable: "Without my husband and my friends encouraging me and reminding me of my capabilities," she said, "I would probably still be stuck in a dead-end job."

Your Network Helps You with Difficult Decisions

Life is an endless series of decisions. Every day you're confronted with decisions about what to wear, what to eat, how to spend your time, and so on. Even seemingly small decisions are often exasperating. A man told us that the worst thing about going out some place special with his wife is trying to decide which clothes are appropriate for the occasion.

Certain decisions—like whether or not to change careers, move to a new house, or place an aging, ill parent in a nursing home—are more difficult than others. This is because they affect the course of your life and the quality of your relationships.

Your social network can be most helpful in the face of such decisions. It can provide:

- A sounding board enabling you to clarify your thoughts

- New insights and perspectives

- Support and encouragement for decisions you need to make

For example Danielle and Seth, an empty-nest couple, felt apprehensive about their son, Jay. They regarded Jay as a financially irresponsible young man. He frequently spent more than he earned and then asked his parents for loans. The loans, however, were never repaid. Danielle and Seth discussed the matter with friends, a couple who'd experienced similar difficulties with their adult child. As a result, they gained both the insight and support they needed to make and follow through with a difficult decision. Seth recalls this trying time:

We were afraid of alienating our son. Our friends knew how we felt because they had experienced similar fears. They helped us realize that we couldn't make a risk-free decision. If Danielle and I kept giving Jay money, he might never become a responsible, independent adult. If we didn't give it to him, he might feel rejected and distance himself from us. There was a risk attached to whatever we decided.

It was this insight that finally helped us make the decision. We'd been looking for a sure-proof solution. But there wasn't one. We decided to tell him that we felt it was in his best interest if we limited what we gave him and that any further loans would depend on the previous ones being paid. So far it's worked well. Jay may not like having strings attached to the money we give him, but he is still a part of our lives.

Your Network Improves Your Health

Both your physical and emotional health benefit from your social network. Researchers who study the effects on health from having friends report a number of benefits. In particular, a strong social network helps:

- Improve overall mental health

- Build and maintain high self-esteem

- Strengthen the body's immune system

- Reduce the risk of colds, high blood pressure, and heart disease

- Keep people feeling and looking younger

One empty-nest father, Tim, shares his experience, illustrating the value of a social network for personal well-being:

I was older when we had our children, so I ended up retiring the same year our last son left home. I love my retirement, but I don't like the way some people treat me—as if I'm over-the-hill. Like I don't have much value to anyone anymore. If I just paid attention to those people, I could really get depressed. I've got a family and a lot of friends who value me for who I am and appreciate what I have to offer. They don't regard me as over-the-hill. My social circle makes me feel good about myself.

Your Network Strengthens You in Times of Crisis

Like a friend, crises come in many varieties. They range from the extraordinary—life-threatening and earthshaking—variety to the more ordinary mixture—the daily difficulties and challenges—that are common to us all. Examples of typical crises can include:

- Facing the empty nest

- Moving to a different area

- Changing jobs or retiring

- Physical or mental illness

- Marital problems

- Death of a loved one

- Financial problems

- Falling out with someone who's been important to you

- Problems your children are having

- Being victimized by a crime

When these kinds of crises occur in your life, your social network can be a crucial factor in helping you cope with the situation.

A single empty-nester, Monica, discovered this when an accident damaged nerves in her arm, requiring extensive physical therapy. She was not only unable to work but also unable to drive herself to the physical therapy sessions. In her pain and frustration, Monica tearfully disclosed her predicament to a friend. Within a few days, her friend gave her a calendar listing the times of her therapy sessions and the names of people who would be driving her to the hospital on each occasion.

Monica's friends provided the physical assistance she needed. They also gave her emotional support; both by their very act of helping and by talking with her as they drove back and forth to the hospital. "They just overwhelmed me with their kindness," she said. They also enabled her to go through the therapy with a minimum of stress and worry.

Take a Moment ...

to recall times when you have faced various crises. Did you try to handle any of them alone? Did you solicit or accept help from your social network for some or all of them? As you look back, what helped you the most in dealing with each of the crises? We hope that your recollections will encourage you to do two things: (1) never hesitate to call on those in your social network when you need help and, (2) be quick to offer help to those in your social network in their times of need.

Your Network Adds Zest to Your Life

In her novel *The Custom of the Country*, Edith Wharton uses the telling phrase, "a desultory dabbling with life (1989: 47)." She is referring to people who never plunge deeply into life in order to know the full range of human emotions and experiences. That's one way to live out your days—just dabbling with life. The very fact that you're reading *this* book indicates that you aren't satisfied with a superficial way of living. You want depth and zest in your life. And, these are qualities that your social network can provide. Here are a few comments about how friends add depth and zest to life:

> My friends, including a few whom I've known since we were children, are tremendously important. They enrich and bring joy into my life.

> I didn't even realize how important friends were until I reached fifty. They're my lifeblood—a rare treasure in my life. My close friends offer new perspectives on life that I trust and respect.

> My friends keep me going. They make me feel secure. They lift my spirits. They make life so much more enjoyable. In fact, the most exciting and delightful experiences in my life have been with my wife and with my friends.

How to Expand Your Social Network

Perhaps you're surrounded by many friends already and only need to intensify a few of those friendships now that the nest is empty. Or perhaps you, like many empty-nesters, are now looking around for new people to add to your social network. Maybe former friends have moved or you've moved. Or you simply didn't maintain many close friendships while you were raising your children. How do you now expand your social network?

Giving Free Rein to Your Creativity

Brainstorm. If you're married, work together to think of ways to meet and cultivate new friends. If you're single, ask one of your children or a relative to brainstorm with you. You can also do it alone. The following ideas can stimulate you to think of other ways to meet people:

- If you belong to an organization—a professional group, a church or synagogue, a political club, or a hobby group—identify an individual or couple you think you'd like to know. Introduce yourself and let the person know what qualities you admire in him or her (for example, "Hi, I'm Jack. I see you here all the time. And I really appreciate that you're always informed on the issues").

- If you don't belong to such an organization, join one that interests you. Most groups host special events designed to introduce members to each other.

- Volunteer for some worthy cause that will enable you to simultaneously reach out and meet new friends.

- Take a continuing education class at a nearby college or university.

- Attend community activities that involve smaller groups (such as book review or foreign affairs discussions).

- Initiate a "get to know your neighbors" program. Invite some people who live near you to your home for a glass of wine or cup of coffee. Find out where each one comes from and what their interests are.

Notice that you can combine the expansion of your social network with reaching out and expanding the self. If you're married, your efforts can also strengthen your couplehood. As Max and Lily discovered, attending to one aspect of your new way of life doesn't mean that you neglect the others:

*Max and I agreed that we needed to strengthen our bonds
with existing friends as well as make some new friends. So we
started a book group. We started with three couples, but today
we have ten couples and two single people. The format has
changed too. We've always dined together as part of our book
discussion evening. But now that the group is so much larger,
we've gone from a sit-down dinner prepared by the evening's
host couple to potluck dinners where everyone brings a
contribution.*

*We've also varied the format. For example, we
occasionally invite in local writers and poets to read from their
works. We've had some lively evenings with these guests. And
once in a while we'll take in a movie together that is an
adaptation of a book we've read.*

*Two years ago we decided to share our love of reading.
We adopted an elementary school library in an improvised area
of our city. Twice a year we contribute books that we have
collected from friends or purchased at book fairs to supplement
the meager fare of this library. And several of our members
also volunteer their time to the school—reading to kindergarten
children and tutoring older children. What started out as a
small book discussion group now fills a large part of our lives.
And we love it!*

The point is, be creative not only in the ways you meet people
but also in the ways you expand your social network to further your
other goals. Few of us have unlimited time even if the nest is empty.
If you can make new friends while also expanding the self or reaching out or strengthening your marriage, go for it!

Look for Compatibility

When joining an organization or engaging in an activity to make
new friends, remember this principle: Avoid bird-watching if birds
bore you. Maybe you practice this principle already. But we know
people who've gotten involved in activities in which they had no
interest other than to meet friends. Not surprisingly, these ventures
usually turn out to be useless at best. This isn't to say you shouldn't
try something new. If you've never attended a political meeting, for
example, you might want to give it a try. Political meetings may be
your grand, undiscovered passion—an opportunity for you to expand
the self and meet new friends. But if you find politics a total bore to

begin with, this probably won't happen. Therefore, pursue organizations and activities that are compatible with your interests.

Similarly, look for people with whom you are compatible. The old saying "opposites attract" is true for magnets but not for people. The more someone is like you in attitudes, ideals, beliefs, interests, and background, the more likely you'll be able to fashion a friendship with that person. Dan, an empty-nest father who moved to a new city because of his work, reported one of his efforts to form friendships:

> *I was at a Chamber of Commerce meeting and I met this guy who was originally from the city where I used to live. I thought we might hit it off, so I asked him what he did. He was an insurance salesman. I have no interest whatever in insurance and didn't know what to say next. He didn't seem to have anything more to say either. So we both just drifted off into conversations with other people.*

Dan took the chance and extended himself, but quickly realized he should probably try to meet someone with whom he had more in common. Compatibility is also the key in establishing new couple friends. However, couple compatibility is an even more complex commodity. Thus, it may be a greater challenge to establish new couple friends than it is to make individual friends. As Katie, an empty-nest mother, observed:

> *We've had a problem finding couple friends. Sometimes I'll really like the woman but my husband finds the man boring. Or my husband is close to the man, but his wife is too extreme for my tastes. We've decided that compatible couples are a rarity.*

Of course, you don't have to be compatible in every way in order to be friends with someone. Yet the greater your compatibility, the more likely it is that your friends will truly enhance the quality of your life.

Take a Moment ...

to write down what you need in a friend. That is, what qualities do you admire in other people? If you had an ideal friend, what kind of person would that friend be? Think about your own ideals and beliefs. How many of those would you like your friend to share? Keep your list in mind as you meet potential new friends. For example, if music is your passion or sports your consuming interest, you'll want to know early in a developing relationship how the other person feels about the matter.

Expect Trial and Error

Developing new friendships is a trial-and-error process. Don't get frustrated or discouraged and stop trying because of initial rejections or aborted efforts. You'll probably experience both hurdles—the rejections and the aborted efforts.

Tanya and Denny experienced rejection while trying to establish friendships in their new community:

We decided to meet the neighbors. In our old neighborhood, people came to greet us when we moved in. Here, no one did. So we took the initiative. The second couple we met seemed like possible friends. But they quickly let us know that they were very busy and had no time for new friends. They weren't that blunt, but we got the point.

Aborted efforts occur because you only learn certain things about others after being around them for a period of time. Although it would be nice, you can't exactly take the list you wrote about your ideals for friends and quiz new people on each item. For example, politics may be very important to you, but you don't normally start a potential new friendship with an in-depth political discussion. Like Rick and Nancy, who are passionate about politics, you may not discover whether you're politically compatible with someone until you've spent some time together:

We met this couple through Rick's work. They moved here recently, and Rick liked the guy immediately. So we invited them over for a drink. We had a great time. We followed it up with the suggestion that we all go out to dinner one night. We did. And by a chance remark, we discovered that we were at opposite ends of the political spectrum. We still like the couple. But they are so morbidly conservative that we just haven't become close friends.

Such things happen. People can form friendships in spite of political or other differences. But Rick and Nancy are so committed to their political beliefs that they need friends who at least hold similar sentiments. They've since found more like-minded friends. But it has been a trial-and-error process.

Take Small Steps

In the trial-and-error process of forming new friendships, patience is not merely a virtue but a necessity. It takes time to become a friend. Friendships crystallize as people open themselves up to each other gradually, finding bonds of commonality.

Rick and Nancy, as we indicated, have found friends with whom they are compatible. One couple lives near them. The process took time and it involved small steps:

> *Rick was coming home from work when he spotted a moving van on a street near our house. On impulse, he drove up, stopped, introduced himself, and welcomed them to the neighborhood. They seemed very pleased. A couple of weeks later, we walked over to their house and dropped in just to see how they were adjusting. They urged us to come in for some coffee. A couple of weeks after that, we invited them to our house to play some board games. Those evenings enabled us to get to know each other better. As we realized how well we all got on, we made more of an effort. Then they invited us for dinner. The upshot is that we have become very good friends. We do things together now. But I would say about three years elapsed from the afternoon when Rick saw them moving in until we could call them good friends.*

Note the small steps—a cordial welcome, a casual visit with a lot of getting to know each other, a dinner, and then additional joint activities. In your eagerness to enlarge your social network, you might be tempted to short-circuit the process. But unfortunately, your enduring friendships will take time to develop.

How to Nurture and Maintain Friendships

Whether your goal is to find and develop new friendships or to deepen existing ones, four methods are particularly useful: practice *gradual self-disclosure; listen;* express *appreciation;* and establish *mutuality.*

Practice Gradual Self-Disclosure

Friendship is an intimate relationship. There can be no intimacy without self-disclosure. An empty-nest mother told us that she gave up on a woman she had hoped to befriend because "although she's very accepting of me and we share a lot of things in common, she never talks about herself. I feel like she knows a lot about me and I know very little about her."

What do you need to know about others, and what do they need to know about you, in order to be friends? Self-disclosure involves sharing feelings, needs, ideas, and beliefs. Sharing such matters makes you vulnerable (which is why we say there needs to be *gradual* self-disclosure). Like Brad, you may find that the other person reacts negatively:

> *I was talking with my friend Louis at work. While we were chatting about a new hire in the firm—a guy who was extremely productive but who was having a hard time getting along with the rest of us—I confessed that at times I was jealous of him because of his productivity. Louis scowled and said he never felt jealousy, only irritation. The way he said it, I knew I shouldn't have admitted my feelings to him. He didn't understand my jealousy. I decided I wouldn't confide in Louis in that way anymore.*

You can't know, of course, whether or not someone is the kind of person who will accept and understand your feelings until you disclose those feelings. But if you disclose yourself gradually, you'll most likely gain a sense of how much you can tell a particular person.

Listen

Friendship is a *dialogue*, not a monologue nor two monologues that periodically interrupt each other. This means that you need to practice the listening skills we discussed in previous chapters as well as self-disclosure with your friends. The failure to listen can impair or even ruin a friendship. Brad had another abortive experience in his quest to find friends:

> *I met Hank when our sons were both in Little League. We got along well and went fishing together frequently. However, we never became intimate friends because Hank only listened when it suited him. He and I had some lively discussions when he was interested in the topic. But if I tried to talk to him about something that I was concerned about, it often seemed like it didn't register in his brain. I still see Hank occasionally.*

But I wouldn't go to him if I really needed to talk to someone about a problem.

Listening is a way to let a person know that you care about him or her. It is a way of saying, "I have a stake in this relationship. I want it to continue." And it invites and encourages the other to continue his or her process of self-disclosure with you.

Express Appreciation

Think about the people you really like to be around. Why do you enjoy being with them? Among other things, they're probably people who appreciate you and who articulate that appreciation.

It's easy to see how expressions of appreciation create warm bonds. Just reflect on how the following statements would make you feel if someone said them to you:

- I really value your friendship.
- You have a wonderful sense of humor.
- What a great idea that is!
- Thank you for listening to me; it's really helped me.
- You are so talented.
- You're the only person I know who takes my dreams seriously.

And so on. Friends, like spouses, need not only to be appreciated but to *hear* your appreciation from time to time.

The husband in an empty-nest couple shared the following story with us:

My wife worked with Frieda and they became good friends. After a few years, my wife left the company but maintained the friendship. Eventually, we got together as couples. We are now all close friends. For many reasons. We have a lot of the same interests. We share the same values. We have a good time when we're together.

Recently they invited us to their house to celebrate a career change that Frieda had made. As we raised our glasses of champagne in toast, Frieda said: "Here's to the best thing that came out of my years in that company—our friendship with the two of you." I know, of course, she got more out of her company than just that, but it really made us feel good to hear that Frieda and Sam value us as much as we value them.

Establish Mutuality

In a friendship, both parties self-disclose, both listen, and both express appreciation. Each is available to the other to fulfill the various functions of friendship. In other words, your friends will do such things as support your growth and help you with difficult decisions, and you will do the same for them.

Like a strong marriage, maintaining strong friendships is a matter of giving as well as receiving. At any time, you might be giving more than you are receiving. In the long run, there will probably be a balance between how much you give and how much you receive. As Elizabeth, a single mother, expressed it:

> When my son got his own apartment, I grew much closer to certain friends. I started doing more things with them. I depended on them to help me with my loneliness. I even depended on them to help me or at least advise me about some minor repairs around the house that my son used to do.
>
> Then one day one of my closest friends called me and said she needed to talk to me because she was agonizing over a decision she needed to make. It took me aback. I guess I thought of myself as being the needy one and my friends as the helpers. Because I was busy when she called, I almost asked if we could wait a day or two. But she sounded desperate. So we arranged to meet.
>
> As I drove to meet her at a coffee shop, I thought to myself that this is what friendship is really all about. You've got to be there for each other, even if it involves some sacrifice. She was always there for me. I had to be there for her, too. In fact, I realized that the tasks I had put aside to be with her weren't nearly as important as she is to me. Our friendship moved to a new level after that day. I was able to help her like she had been helping me. It felt really good.

Reflecting and Planning

Although we've focused on friends, remember your social network also includes family members. Assess the adequacy of your network. Write down the names of people to whom you can comfortably turn to meet the following needs:

- Companionship

- Confidential conversations

- Guidance for a troublesome issue

- Help in making a decision

- Emotional support in time of crisis

- Encouragement for new ventures

- Sharing a social occasion—going to the movies, a party, attending a concert, etc.

- Taking occasional vacations or trips

- Day-to-day intimacy

Ideally, you should have a number of people available for such needs. As you look at the previous list, are there some needs for which you have a weak or inadequate network? Are there some needs for which you would like to expand your network?

Assuming that you are interested in a larger network, take stock of your existing network. First, think of any relatives with whom you would like to have a closer relationship. Second, think about your present friends. Would you like to deepen your relationship with any of them?

You may be able to expand your social network simply by deepening your existing relationships. But you'll probably want to expand it to include new people as well. Use the suggestions in this chapter and keep the following in mind:

- Set a goal (e.g., I will meet one new person this month).

- Take steps to meet the goal—don't leave it to chance.

- Incorporate your other goals of expanding the self and reaching out. What can you do that will address these goals and also give you the opportunity to expand your social network?

- Remind yourself that making friends is a trial-and-error process. Don't get discouraged and quit if your first efforts fail to result in a new friend.

- For various reasons (e.g., people move and people change) you may need to repeat the process. Assess your social network periodically.

- Remember that friends are invaluable and worth the effort it takes to make and cultivate them.

Part III

Complications

Life is difficult.

—M. Scott Peck

10

When Your Nest Gets Cluttered Again

Imagine yourself having come to terms with your children leaving the nest. Imagine yourself setting out on a new and exciting dimension of life. Imagine yourself having new adventures as you do things you haven't had time for in the past. You're happy and enthusiastic about life.

Now imagine two scenarios. In the first, you've prepared yourself for the empty nest and are anticipating the adventures awaiting you after your children leave home. The time comes. But your last child announces that he or she is *not* going away to college after all. Your child has decided to spend the next four years at home while attending a local university.

In the second scenario, your last child has left home and you're enjoying your freedom. You have plans. You have new activities. You're following a different schedule. One day, you answer a knock at the door. It is your child. "Hi, mom. I'm back!"

Is any of this unrealistic? Not in the least! In fact, there's a good chance that your anticipated empty-nest life will be delayed or impeded. Your nest may remain cluttered longer than you expected or become filled again after an interval of emptiness. It's important to know how to deal with the situation.

How Many Nests Remain Cluttered and Why?

How many nests remain cluttered after parents had expected them to be empty? Why do children remain home longer than anticipated, or return after they presumably have left the nest? The answers to these questions will give you some idea of what you can expect to happen in your own nest.

What Are Your Chances?

Research has shown that you have about a 50–50 chance (and it may be rising) that one or more of your children will either remain at home after you expected them to leave or will return home after having left. According to government data, close to half of all parents in the forty-five to fifty-four-year-old age range have an adult child living at home (U.S. Bureau of Census 1997: 58).

A national survey of young adults (ages nineteen to thirty-four) who left the parental nest found that 42.4 percent of them returned home at least once. Sons were more likely (46.2 percent) than daughters (38.9 percent) to return home. More than half of those returning did so within two years of leaving home. About two-thirds stayed at home for a year or less, but one out of ten remained for four or more years (Aquilino 1996).

Nor is the cluttering experience necessarily ended once the returning child has left again. About a fourth of those who return do so more than once. Thus, a little over 10 percent of adult children (often those who were never adequately prepared to leave in the first place) bounce back and forth between the parental home and other homes.

Why Do They Do It?

There are a number of reasons why adult children remain in the nest long after you expected it to be empty. Here are some typical reasons for children coming back home:

- Need a place to live while establishing themselves financially in a career

- Want to live with family until they marry and establish a family of their own

- Have lost their job

- Are recovering from a divorce

- Are a single parent and need the assistance of family

- Have difficulty functioning independently

- Have suffered traumatic experiences that require a secure base while regaining perspective and/or stability

You are no doubt more comfortable with some of these reasons than others. But all of them happen. Financial reasons are particularly common.

Many young people complete their college education heavily in debt and are unable to secure a high-paying job. If faced with re-payment of student loans, high rent or mortgages, and the other financial responsibilities of adult life, they may feel trapped in a cycle of increasing debt. Not surprisingly, living at home is an attractive solution to their financial problems.

Relational problems are also common. Children may return home after a divorce. Because the financial resources of divorced women frequently drop significantly after a divorce, a divorced daughter may find herself in financial straits. If she has children, she may need parental help—both emotional and other kinds of support—as she rebuilds her life.

Mae, a widowed mother whose daughter experienced a series of traumatic events, tells why it was important for her daughter to return home:

> *My daughter Kathy was living with a man she planned
> to marry. But he decided that he wasn't ready to commit.
> He moved out and moved in with another woman. My
> daughter was left with the responsibility of paying the full
> rent for their apartment. She struggled along for a while, but
> then lost her job when her company downsized. Within a few
> weeks, Kathy's savings had dwindled considerably and she
> still hadn't found another job. I urged her to return home.
> Although she didn't want to give up her own place, she
> didn't have much choice. She was desperate.*
>
> *We're doing well together. I think both of us enjoy being
> together again. We both know, however, that it's important for
> her to be independent. So as soon as she finds another job, she
> plans to move into her own apartment.*

Mae and her daughter are handling the situation in a responsible, loving way. They have adjusted to a cluttered nest with minimal upset. It isn't always that easy.

Take a Moment ...

to evaluate the prospect, using the reasons previously given, that your children will move back home at some point. If your nest is empty, what are the chances that you'll experience a cluttered nest at some time in the future? Of course, you can't predict something like job loss or divorce. Still, if you have a sense that you'll be one of the many parents with an adult child at home, read on so you can be as prepared as possible.

If your nest is cluttered now, which of the reasons apply to your situation? If you believe your child is unprepared for independent living, you and/or your child may need counseling. If there are other reasons, the materials in this chapter should help you make the experience a positive one for both you and your child.

The Consequences of a Cluttered Nest

As Mae and her daughter Kathy learned, a nest that is refilled for a short time can be a positive experience. Unfortunately, a lot of negative consequences can also occur. The following are seven common consequences.

1. *Regression to the earlier dependent relationship stage and stagnation:* When a child returns home, some families regress, or try to regress, to their earlier relationship—when the children were dependent and the parents assumed responsibility for them. This means a regression from the ways of relating to adult children that we discussed in chapters 4 and 5 and reverting to patterns you had when your children were adolescents.

   For example, Tony and Carol were quite willing for their out-of-work, single son to return to the nest until he could get another job. But they fell into a pattern of relating to him as they had when he was in high school. Thus, Tony felt perfectly free to tell his son what time to be in at night, and was angry when his son ignored the curfew. And Carol set a place at the dinner table each night and was hurt when her son didn't eat with them. "He didn't tell us that he was dining with friends," she complained. "He just didn't show up."

The result of regression, then, is likely to be parent-child misunderstandings and conflict. It also is likely to stagnate your own growth. If you regress, you won't be relating to your child as an adult. And you'll be putting the time and energy into parenting that should be devoted to other pursuits.

2. *Loss of privacy:* One of the more common aspects of the cluttered nest for parents is the loss of privacy. They no longer feel as free to do what pleases them in their own home. One empty-nest couple, Michelle and David, were disappointed in this development:

> *We really enjoyed being free about sex again. We could be cuddling on the couch watching television and decide to have sex. Now we're back to waiting until our daughter is asleep or away somewhere.*

3. *Financial strain:* Children who return home sometimes contribute to family expenses and sometimes do not. In either case, their parents are likely to encounter additional expenses. At a minimum, a child in the home means higher utility bills, food bills, laundry costs, and wear and tear on furnishings and automobiles. There also may be additional expenses for clothing, insurance, transportation, entertainment, and so forth.

At the very least, these additional costs will reduce the amount you have for pursuing the new dimension of life you anticipated as an empty-nester. In the worst of cases, you'll find yourself going into debt in order to subsidize your child's presence in the home.

Moreover, when there is added financial strain, old patterns and conflicts will tend to crop up again—financial strain may result in regression to an earlier stage. You might, for example, find yourself shouting at your child to turn off the lights when he or she leaves a room. You might get angry if you see your child wasting food. You might resent your child using the family car when he or she could have walked somewhere or taken a bus. Your child is an adult, but financial strain has pushed you back to an earlier stage of your relationship.

4. *Increased tasks and demands:* Depending on what kind of arrangements you set up, the increase in the number of tasks and demands you experience can vary from minimal to overwhelming. Jane, a mother of three, found the increase almost unbearable. She had a demanding job. Until her children left home, she had almost

no time for pursuing personal interests. Once her children were on their own, she and her husband had the time and freedom to do things like garden. She loves flowers: "My soul resonates with them."

The change began with their oldest daughter. She moved back home after college and brought her cat with her. Then Jane's son, who lived in another state, decided he wanted to live and work in her city and moved back home until he could find work. He brought his dog with him. Jane and her husband suddenly grew from a couple to four people and two pets. It quickly became a nightmare. She remembers:

> *Instead of my husband or me picking up something for dinner on the way home, I found myself cooking for five. Instead of tending my garden and reading a book after dinner, I found myself in the midst of family activities. It seemed that the house was always a mess. The dog nearly ruined my garden. I found the cat on the table one evening licking the butter. I was always dealing with the pets as well as the children. I love my children dearly, but I'd just as soon forget the year they were all back home.*

5. *Increased worries:* In some ways, ignorance really is bliss. If you don't know about your child's problems, you won't worry about them. A father summed up the virtue of not knowing:

> *Frankly, unless my son needs my help there's a lot I don't want to know. I prefer to remain ignorant. He's very competent. He can deal with his problems. My worry won't help him and it certainly won't help me.*

The problem is, when a child is back in the nest, it's almost impossible not to know. And knowledge is worrisome. In fact, as parents in a cluttered nest know from experience, the opportunities for worrying when a child returns home are almost limitless:

- If the child's marriage has broken up, you worry about his or her recovery and potential for a future stable relationship.

- If the child is unemployed, you worry about him or her securing meaningful work.

- If the child needs support while gathering sufficient resources to become independent, you worry about how well the process is going and how long it will take.

- If the child is out late at night, you worry about his or her safety until you hear the door open.

- If you believe your child isn't eating well-balanced meals, you worry about his or her health.

- If your child is lax about helping around the house, you worry about his or her sense of responsibility.

To be sure, most of these worries are needless because your children are perfectly capable of managing their own lives. Yet you probably can't avoid worrying when your child and your child's problems are living with you.

6. *Complications for schedules and routines:* We know many parents who feel fragmented and weary from juggling the complex schedules of two or more children. You may have thought this was all behind you. But when an adult child returns home, you may find that your schedules and routines conflict with those of your child. Like the harried mother who found herself cooking for five again, you may find yourself adjusting schedules and routines that have become quite comfortable for you.

   Some of these scheduling conflicts include:

   - Meal times and meal preparation
   - Time for viewing television or playing the stereo
   - Household tasks, such as laundry and cleaning
   - Routine activities, such as the parents' date night
   - Use of such things as automobiles and computers
   - Respecting each other's privacy

7. *Strained relationships:* In the light of all the above, it's not surprising that there can be strained relationships when the nest becomes cluttered again. Parents complain that their adult children are insensitive to their needs, take too much for granted, and don't assume their fair share of household tasks. Children frequently complain of encroachments on their freedom and of interference in their lives.

   A cluttered nest can also put a strain on your marital relationship. These strains arise for a number of reasons. You may find yourself with less time for your relationship and resent your children for this. You may also resent the additional work and worry. Another common source of marital strain is disagreement over how to deal with the adult child who has returned home. Typically, one spouse thinks that the other is being too hard or too easy on the child and vice versa. A woman whose marriage nearly broke up over the issue relates:

After our daughter graduated from college, she moved back home until she could find a good job. After a year, she found one but quit it after a few months. She didn't think there was any future in it for her. I was furious. But my husband said I was too harsh with her. He said he was quite happy to have her stay home until she found what she was looking for. We could afford it, so why not?

I reminded him that we had started out with less than ideal jobs. I also reminded him that most of the burden of the extra work of having our daughter at home fell on me. Then he started telling me about the nature of the job market, and I really hit the ceiling. He acted as if the real problem was that I was too ignorant of economic reality to understand why our daughter needed to stay in our house.

Fortunately, their daughter eventually found work and moved out. Unfortunately, this couple experienced an intense strain. They ended up in counseling and have now worked through the issue. "We came very close to splitting up," the wife comments. "I'm grateful we didn't. I just hope that other couples who have a child move back home are aware of the dangers involved."

We need to balance this litany of adverse consequences by noting that the returning child can also provide an opportunity for building a better relationship. When parents provide needed support for an adult child, they have the opportunity to strengthen the parent-child bond.

A returning child can also give you time to make up for spending inadequate time with your child in earlier years. Brett, an empty-nest father, was delighted when his son spent a year at home while trying to get a business started:

I spent too many hours at work when Joel was young. We didn't do a lot of things that other fathers and sons do together. It never hit me how much I missed all that until he left. When he came back, it gave me a chance to get to know him in a way I hadn't known him before. It was tough at first. I didn't realize how much he resented my neglect of him. But by year's end, I think we had developed a good relationship. It's still developing. All this might never have happened if he hadn't come home.

Whatever the nature of your relationship with your children while they were growing up, a child returning can be a strained experience, or an opportunity for enhancing the quality of the relationship. If it's to be the latter, you need to implement the following suggestions.

How to Survive and Thrive in a Cluttered Nest

Assumptions are the enemy of good relationships. Therefore, when your child returns to the nest, do *not assume* that you each will know how to adjust and make the situation workable. Families get into trouble precisely because everyone assumes that thoughtful preparation and discussion aren't required. If you are to survive and even thrive in your cluttered nest, attend to the following five principles.

Practice Open Communication

Open doesn't mean transparent. You may, for instance, have reservations about a child returning home that you won't want to tell him or her. You may, after the child is home, experience transient moments of irritation that you won't verbalize. It isn't necessary to lift the shade of your inner being and expose every thought and feeling to your family. Rather, open communication means that each member of the family is honest about feelings, expectations, and needs.

For example, do you assume that your child will be present each evening at dinner? Tell your child that you have that expectation. If the child agrees that he or she will usually have dinner with you, ask your child to let you know in advance when he or she is not going to be there. You can promise to do the same when you will be away.

Similarly, you should be able to say to your child and your child should be able to say to you such things as: "I'm feeling weary. I need some quiet time to myself." Or: "I'm sorry I'm irritable. I've had a rough day at work—it has nothing to do with you." Or: "When you don't pick up your clothes, it adds to my workload. I need your help on this." And you'll also want to share positive matters: "Thanks for preparing the dinner tonight. It really helps me." Or: "I really appreciate that you filled the car with gas after you used it this weekend. I never have enough time on Monday morning to fill the tank."

Take a Moment ...

to list the expectations you have for a child living with you again. Read over the complications in schedules and routines. What would you expect of your child on each of those items? Often people have conflict because their expectations are violated; they assume that the other knows their expectations even though they haven't communicated them. If a child returns home, be ready to discuss and negotiate your expectations. If your child is at home now, are you having strain or conflict because one or more of your expectations is being violated? If so, make sure that you let your child know what you expect. Then be prepared to negotiate.

Establish Shared Understandings

This could easily read establish "rules." But the notion of rules for an adult child seems incongruous to us. We prefer to talk about *shared understandings*. Certainly, you create a healthier atmosphere when you talk about shared understandings rather than the rules of the house.

You need to have a set of shared understandings from the time your child first returns home. This will keep you from acting at cross-purposes or getting mired in irritation when your expectations aren't met. As you establish shared understandings, be sure to address the following:

- Who will be responsible for various household chores

- When each family member can use such things as the automobile, the computer, and the telephone

- Activities you may or may not want in your home (e.g., parties where there is heavy alcohol or other drug use, smoking, or sexual partners staying overnight)

- Activities that help your child to establish independence (e.g., regular job hunting, attending a divorce recovery group, or saving money)

- Ways to insure the privacy needs of every family member

- Care, feeding, and any restrictions on a pet your child brings home

- How much, if any, financial support you'll provide for your child

- How much room and board your child will pay, and how much your child will contribute toward other household expenses

Deciding how much to charge your child for room and board can be troublesome. Some parents believe it unnecessary to ask a child to pay room and board or to contribute to household expenses. They feel that this is the child's home, and he or she is welcome to return at anytime.

However, other parents argue that there is value in letting a child share household expenses. It reminds the adult child that your resources are not unlimited, reinforces the need for personal responsibility, and encourages a more rapid move toward independence. Many even advocate a written rental agreement. In this case, you'll need to work out an amicable and fair arrangement with your child. As you do, keep in mind that you don't want to make the payments so high that they delay your child's move to independence.

And what if you're not sure whether it is best to ask your child to contribute or not? We believe the answer depends on how you feel, how the child feels, the nature of your relationship, and the situation. If an answer evades you, we suggest that you talk to a counselor or a trusted friend. They can't make the decision for you, but they can help you gain the needed insight to make a decision.

Maintaining Mutual Respect

Maintaining mutual respect is relating to each other as adults along the lines we discussed in chapters 4 and 5. One of the first steps in establishing mutual respect is carefully listening to your child's reasons for and feelings about coming home. Avoid saying anything suggesting you're berating or blaming. Just listen so that you understand.

Listening also means that you won't be satisfied with a quick answer like, "I need to stay here until I find a job." You both need to understand such things as your child's:

- Feelings about the situation that led to him or her coming home

- Feelings about being back at home

- Sense of how long he or she might need to stay

- Sense of his or her needs and expectations during the time at home

- Plans for becoming independent again

Your task is to understand and support your child rather than to solve his or her problems. Because your life is taking a direction you didn't anticipate or prefer, it may be difficult to resist trying to find a quick fix to whatever problem brought the child home. Nevertheless, in order to make the experience a positive one for everyone, it's essential that you respect your child as an adult.

Of course, this means that your child must also respect you as an adult. Your child should respect the new life you have carved out for yourself and should not expect you to take over all past parental duties. Phyllis, a single mother whose son returned home between jobs, found it necessary to be explicit about what she could and could not do:

> *Keith goes out at night with his friends. Sometimes he stays with one of them overnight. I told him I would like to know when he's going to do that. I also told him that there are times when I work late or have a meeting or a social engagement, so I would not be fixing all his meals. Sometimes I would like for him to prepare dinner for both of us. And I also asked him to do his own laundry and help with other chores around the house.*
>
> *This way he respects my needs. And I respect his. I don't ask him where he's going every time he leaves the house. I don't nag him about finding a job; I know he's trying. And if he asks to borrow a little money, I don't ask him what he wants it for. I trust him.*

Phyllis and her son are doing well together because each respects the other as an adult. They will probably look back on this time as a pleasant interlude rather than a troublesome episode.

Encouraging Independence

Wittingly or unwittingly, it's possible for you to prolong your child's return visit. Answer the following questions honestly:

- Do I enjoy my child being home again because I have been lonely without him or her?

- Is my marriage better when my child is home than when he or she is gone?

- Am I making it easy for my child to be dependent by giving too much financial support?

- Am I undercutting my child's initiative by giving too much sympathy?

- Do I foster irresponsibility in my child by doing tasks that he or she should be doing?

If the answer is yes to any of these, you need to alter your behavior so that you encourage independence rather than dependence. Parents have encouraged independence by such things as:

- Setting a time limit on how long the child can remain at home (a limit which is not inflexible, however)

- Giving a child responsibility for various household tasks

- Requiring the child to pay a portion of the household expenses

- Encouraging a child to take a job that is less than ideal in order to become self-supporting

- Helping a child with an initial payment on an apartment

- Helping a child furnish an apartment so that he or she can afford to move

- Teaching a child skills that the child needs in order to live independently

- Encouraging any indication the child gives of moving toward independence

Reframing the Situation as Reaching Out

What better way can you reach out than to help a young person regroup and get a fresh start in life? So reframe your child's return home as an opportunity for you to reach out. You are reaching out to someone who needs help. And the help you give can enable that person—who happens to be your child—to get through a difficult time and move on to a better life.

Reflecting and Planning

If you haven't had a child move back home, reflect on the materials in this chapter and mentally prepare yourself in case it happens to you. Even if your children have been gone for some time, it can happen. We have known children to move back after ten years or more of being out of the nest. And even if your children are married with families, it can happen. We know of one case where a man moved back to the parental home with his wife and three children because he had lost his job and was unable to keep up the mortgage payments on his house.

If you now have a child back in the nest, how would you evaluate the experience so far? On a scale of one to ten, where one means you're completely dissatisfied with the situation and ten means you're completely satisfied, what number would you select?

Now answer the question of what needs to happen for your rating to improve. Using the information in this chapter and other ideas you have, write down some specific changes that would make you more satisfied with the arrangement. Set a time with your child to sit down and discuss your ideas. Work together to make the situation as satisfying as possible for everyone.

11

The Sandwich Generation: Caring for Your Aging Parents

"Empty nest?" Adam sounded exasperated as he said it. "It may be empty but we've got as many demands on us as we've ever had. Maybe even more." Adam and Fran had their two children when they were in their late thirties. By the time the children left home, Fran's widowed mother had become increasingly unable to care for herself. Because Fran was an only child, her mother depended heavily upon her daughter and son-in-law to help her with everyday tasks.

Like most other couples, Adam and Fran had anticipated a much different scenario once their children were out of the nest. Yet like many other empty-nesters, they found themselves with a new set of responsibilities—caring for parents.

Who's in the Sandwich Generation?

The *sandwich generation* usually refers to parents who are still in the child-rearing years and also faced with the challenge of caring for aging and ill parents. This definition, however, can be too narrow. We expand the definition in this chapter. We also offer suggestions to help you assess your chances of being caught up in the sandwich generation.

Are You a Candidate?

Do you have some, most, or all of the responsibilities of caring for one or more parents or relatives? If so, you are in the sandwich generation if you're also:

- Heavily involved with your children (e.g., they live near you and spend time with you)

- Supporting your children to some extent financially

- Living in a cluttered nest

- A grandparent and helping raise your grandchildren

You may still be involved in your children's lives even though they no longer live at home. If they're away at college, they may still spend holidays and summers with you. If they live nearby, they may flit in and out of your lives on a regular basis. And so they continue to fill some of your hours, occupy your thoughts, and frequently cause you moments of worry and anxiety.

What Are Your Chances?

So what are your chances of being a part of the sandwich generation? They're actually pretty high. Research has shown the following to be true (National Education Association 1994; Cox 1993: 531):

- A fifth or more of people over the age of seventy need some kind of help with the tasks of living—meals, shopping, transportation, bathing.

- A fourth of all Americans, at some point, will be a caregiver for an aging parent or other relative.

- The average American woman will spend a greater portion of her life caring for aging parents than she spent caring for her children.

- One out of ten grandparents functions as a parent for a period of time.

- A small proportion of grandparents end up raising their grandchildren.

There are a number of reasons for these research findings. More people are living longer. Americans aged seventy-five years and above comprise the fastest growing age group in recent decades. Unfortunately, because of chronic and debilitating diseases many of the aged live a number of years in poor health and in need of assistance.

Women are more likely than men to assume these caregiving responsibilities. Although the number of male caregivers is rising, about three-fourths of all caregivers of aging parents and relatives are women (a substantial number of whom also work outside the home).

Divorce or drug use by parents are the major reasons that grandparents assume the responsibilities of parenting. Another, though less likely, reason is the death of a parent or parents.

Overall, then, millions of Americans find themselves caring for aging parents or other relatives while also having responsibilities for children and/or grandchildren. If you're one of them, you're a part of the sandwich generation. If your parents or your spouse's parents are still living but you have no caretaking responsibilities as yet, we suggest you read this chapter or save it for future reference. Even if your parents live far away, there is a possibility that you'll find yourself faced with the responsibility for their care at some point.

Take Vera, for example. Vera is a West Coast empty-nester. Her mother lived with Vera's older sister on the East Coast. Vera didn't give much thought to caretaking responsibilities until her sister called one day and said, "I'm going crazy with this. I need your help." Vera brought her mother to her home and is now taking care of her.

Experiencing the Sandwich

Throughout this book, we've discussed the adventure awaiting you with the empty nest. Does getting caught in the sandwich mean that you're no longer engaged in that adventure? Not necessarily. Some people assume that caring for an aged parent involves many burdens and few benefits. However, most aged parent–adult child relationships involve mutual help of various kinds. In fact, unless your parent is a complete ingrate, you may end up receiving more than you're giving.

Still, as the caregiving responsibilities increase, it may be difficult to define your situation in a positive way. As we discuss what's involved with being sandwiched, we begin with the challenges and negative aspects. But we will come back to the potential benefits.

Increased Demands

Perhaps the most obvious results of being a caregiver are the increased demands on your time, energy, and resources. Depending on the state of health and financial circumstances of the person or persons for whom you are caring, you could find yourself assisting with:

- Household chores
- Living expenses
- Transportation
- Household repairs
- Daily living activities—eating, dressing, bathing, and shopping

In many ways, caregiving is like being the parent of a dependent child again. But more so—a dependent child becomes increasingly independent. An aged parent becomes increasingly dependent. And the only release comes from getting help from other sources (which can make you feel guilty), placing your parent in a nursing home (we'll discuss this in more detail later in this chapter), or your parent's death. Thus, to be sandwiched means you face a number of possibilities, none of which may be desirable. With such a dismal set of alternatives for the future, it is little wonder that people in the sandwich generation agonize about their situation.

Time Pressure

A sense of time pressure accompanies the additional demands. There is time pressure in a twofold sense. First, you never seem to have enough time to do everything you feel you both ought to do and want to do. Caregiving is time-consuming. The majority of those giving care to an aged parent spend at least four hours a day and as many as seven days a week with their responsibilities.

In other words, caregiving can range from a half-time to a full-time job! Some people quit their jobs in order to meet their caregiving responsibilities. Fran hasn't quit her job, but she's feeling the pressure intensely:

I don't want to stop working. It's actually a relief for me to go into work. But I don't know how much longer I can keep it up. I have a husband who needs me. We have children and grandchildren with whom we want to spend time. And I know I'm not giving any of them enough time since I'm doing so many things for my mother.

It's a damned-if-you-do and damned-if-you-don't situation. If I try to cut back on what I do for Mom, or think about hiring someone to take care of her, I feel guilty. And if I keep doing it myself, I begin to resent the amount of time and effort she takes.

As Fran struggles with trying to find time to meet all her responsibilities each week, she's also fretting about time pressure in another way. Namely, the years of her life are passing by and she doesn't have time for the many things she dreamed of doing when her children left home. Instead of exploring her options, she is doing various chores in her mother's apartment. At times, Fran wonders how old and how fit she'll be when her caretaking days are over.

Anger, Resentment, and Guilt

People who are sandwiched typically can experience anger, resentment, and guilt. The anger and resentment arise from having your expectations thwarted and your dreams delayed for an indefinite time. The heavier the responsibilities, the more likely you'll feel the anger and resentment. Kara, who put her career on hold to spend all of her time caring for her mother, expressed her feelings this way:

I'm to the point where I feel like I don't have a life. My mother called me so often and was so worried about being alone that it seemed easier to resign from my position and keep her with me for a while. But when the time comes, I don't know if I'll be able to resume my career—it's already been two years since I left my job. At times I'm angry with everyone and everything because this has happened to me.

Even if your responsibilities are not as all-consuming, you might feel angry and resentful at the amount of time you spend with your parent—especially if the parent takes what you do for granted and is insensitive to your personal needs. Helene, a woman who spends many hours each week caring for her father, said that the worst part is that he is "either unaware of how much this costs me or he doesn't care. He just takes it for granted that it's what I'm supposed to do."

This anger and resentment can be compounded by feelings of guilt. You might feel guilty simply because you get angry and resent the time you spend caregiving. You might feel guilty about the intensity of your anger—like one woman who said at times she wanted to grab her mother and shake her. You might feel guilty because you're not sure you're doing enough. And you might feel guilty because your parent is manipulative and actually tries to make you feel guilty. This is the experience of Ellen who has been caring for her father for several years:

> *All my life he let me know what it meant to be a "good daughter." If I didn't attend to his needs and wants, I wasn't a good daughter. Now he plays on that by reminding me how old he is, how sick he is, how important it is for me to be there to help him. He asks me to do things for him that I know he's capable of doing himself. If I do them, I resent it. If I don't do them, I feel guilty. I can't win.*

Stress

People who are sandwiched between their children and an aging parent report feeling stressed both physically and emotionally. Physical stress occurs when you overextend yourself caring for a parent, or injure yourself doing such things as lifting a parent or pushing him or her in a wheelchair. Emotional stress comes from the combination of putting much of your life on hold while caring for your parent and watching your parent's deterioration. A woman caring for her mother said that the word she would use is *overwhelmed*:

> *My mother gets depressed. She talks about all the things she can't do anymore. She gets to the point where she doesn't want to eat or leave the house. So I have to try to cheer her up, insist that she eat something, and take her shopping or sightseeing. After a few days, she feels better again. But by that time, I'm utterly exhausted. And all I can think about is, how long will it be until the next bout?*

It's stressful to see a parent sink into a listless depression. It's also stressful to see a parent grow increasingly helpless and dependent. Recall the story of Vera who brought her mother from the East

Coast to live with her. Vera finds that the most stressful part of caregiving is witnessing her mother's loss of control:

When she began wetting the bed, I was angry at first. But I knew she couldn't help it. I put her in diapers. She finds it humiliating. I feel badly, but when I get up at night to change her bedding, I can't get back to sleep. I have to be able to sleep through the night or I won't be able to keep this up.

Finally, caregiving is stressful because it can be isolating. Paul, a man who spends hours each week with his father, said:

It's a lonely task. My father can't hear anymore. He also had a stroke, so he can't talk well. Most of the time that I'm with him, he just sits and stares outside. Or he sleeps. And I simply sit and look at him remembering the man he once was.

Loss of Your Role

Sandwiched people often lose a valued role. The parent may no longer relate to you as a son or daughter—you're simply a caretaker. You're now parenting your parent, and this is a loss. It's comforting to be a child—even an adult child. It's comforting to know that there's someone who cherishes you, supports you, cares about you, and who has resources that are always available to you. When someone on whom you could always count for help and support is unable to provide those things anymore, you feel the loss. In this sense, your role as a child is ended. And for many in the sandwich generation, this loss occurs before the death of the parent.

Rewards

However, the news is not all grim. You can also experience rewards in caring for an aging parent. Some of the rewards identified by caretakers include:

- Increased intimacy
- Opportunities to give something back to parents
- Chance to draw on the parent's wisdom
- New perspectives on life
- Increased patience
- Enhanced self-worth

In fact, most people experience a mixture of the rewards and liabilities of being sandwiched. Even if you feel an increased intimacy with your parent, for example, it doesn't mean you'll never get angry or frustrated or resentful. The challenge is to handle the situation in such a way that the rewards outweigh the negative aspects.

Take a Moment . . .

to think about the rewards you would like to achieve from caring for an aging parent. In what ways could this experience benefit you in terms of how you feel about yourself; your personal growth; your relationship with your parent; and your relationships generally? One way to respond is to put yourself on the other side of the experience—how do you want to look back on it? For example, one woman said:

> *I want to be able to say that I acted in such a way that my mother knew I loved her. When I feel overwhelmed by the frustrations from caregiving, I think about the fact that this will not go on forever. I want to be able to feel good about myself for what I did for her. And I want to feel that we grew closer to each other because it was a special time for both of us.*

To gain such rewards, you need to know how to be an effective caregiver.

How to Be a Caregiver

As we discuss the principles of being an effective caregiver, keep in mind that you can still experience times of frustration, anger, resentment, guilt, weariness, and stress. The principles for effective caregiving won't eliminate all the negative aspects of being sandwiched, but they will enable you to make the overall experience a rewarding one.

Resolving Your Lingering Issues

If you've had a strained relationship with your parent, try to resolve the issues early in the caregiving process. If a parent pushes your guilt button, for example, you can firmly say something like: "When you say that, it makes me feel guilty. I don't want to do this out of guilt but out of love. I need you to help me by not saying such things." Of course, a parent who has had decades of practice in generating guilt probably won't stop after one such request. You may have to remind your parent a number of times: "That's another one of those guilt-producing statements."

It may not be possible to reconcile such issues with your parent. Your parent may be incapable, emotionally, intellectually, or physically, of dealing with it. You may then have no choice but to practice the forgiveness we discussed in chapters 5 and 8. An empty nest mother, Beatrice, grew up with a verbally and emotionally abusive mother. She used the insights and support she gained in therapy to deal with the hurt her mother inflicted:

> *I was getting ready to go to work when the telephone rang. My father had died of a heart attack. I'd distanced myself from my parents, but now I faced the fact that I had to do something about my mother. She suffered from a crippling arthritis that left her in chronic pain and unable to do anything for herself.*
>
> *Fortunately, my mother was willing to have outside help come in so she could stay in her house. That meant that I wouldn't be totally responsible for taking care of her. But I would still have a lot more contact with her than I have had for many years. And I'd have to pick up on some of those tasks that my father had been doing for her.*
>
> *I can't talk to my mother about the way she raised me. She always has the excuse that she's in too much pain. And maybe she is. From my therapy, I learned I had to find a way to get over my own hurt. I began by accepting the fact that I couldn't change my mother. She was always a cold, angry woman, and her arthritis only seemed to make her worse. I also had to give up the hope that someday she would approve of me. I grew up believing that I deserved her abuse, that I was a bad child, and that's why she rejected me. I still struggle with that, but I've given up the need for her approval.*
>
> *Now that I'm taking care of her, I'm relating to her as an adult. It isn't my ideal mother-daughter relationship, but I guess it's about as intimate as it's ever been. And as it ever will be.*

Although Beatrice doesn't use the term "forgiveness" in her account, the process she describes is one of forgiveness—accepting her mother as she is, foregoing any vengeance or retaliation, and letting go of the hurt. An even more satisfying outcome might have resulted if she and her mother could have talked together about the past, and if her mother had been capable of relating to her in a more kindly fashion. Under the circumstances, however, Beatrice did the best she could in resolving lingering issues—she forgave.

Taking Care of Yourself

An unfortunately common mistake among caregivers is to get so enmeshed in caring for someone else that they don't take care of themselves. Taking care of yourself means that you continue to:

- Eat properly.

- Get sufficient rest.

- Get enough exercise.

- Engage in activities that are enjoyable and meaningful for you.

- Gather information about your parent's condition so that you can feel competent.

- Recognize and accept the limits of what you can do.

- Make use of available resources.

- Recognize the signs of, and take steps to deal with, stress in your life.

In upcoming sections we offer specific steps you can take to follow through with many of these points. For now, try to understand what is involved in taking care of yourself in a general sense. With regard to stress, periodically ask yourself the following questions:

- Am I more short-tempered—do little things irritate and frustrate me?

- Am I having frequent or intense times of anger, frustration, resentment, or guilt related to my parent?

- Do I tend to make cutting remarks to my parent?

- Do I frequently feel exhausted?

- Am I often depressed?

- Am I often afflicted with feelings of guilt about my caregiving?

- Do I feel increasingly cut off from other people?

- Am I doing less well at my job?

- Have any of my relationships with family, friends, or colleagues deteriorated?

- Is that deterioration somehow tied to my caregiving responsibilities?

If you answer "yes" to one or more of the questions on this list, you aren't taking care of yourself.

Take a Moment . . .

to evaluate yourself in terms of the questions regarding stress. Of course, there may be other reasons than your caregiving that led you to answer "yes" to the questions. Be honest about your answers; then ask yourself whether any "yes" answers are a direct or indirect result of your caregiving responsibilities. For example, if you work, you may have a new boss with whom you don't get along. Perhaps your deteriorating work performance is tied to that rather than to your caregiving. Or a relationship may have been deteriorating already, and the caregiving simply hastened the process. If your "yes" answers are veritably related to your caregiving, ask yourself what you need to do to take better care of yourself. Review the first list in the "Taking Care of Yourself" section for areas on which you may need to focus.

Caregivers can easily ignore the signs of stress on the grounds that they have no choice in the matter. You always have choices; we'll discuss some of them in the next sections. Moreover, if you don't take care of yourself, you can't adequately take care of someone else as Cora, who cares for her elderly mother, discovered:

Fortunately, I retired early, before I began to take care of my mother. So work is one battle I didn't have. But I had plenty of others. My mother was put on a new medication and turned out to be allergic to it. She had terrible diarrhea. I had to get up two or three times during the night, clean her up, and change her bedding. She was crying because she was so embarrassed. When the doctors switched her medication, she had other problems. In one six-month period, she was in and out of the hospital three different times.

While this was going on, I had several bouts of illness. I was going to the doctor as often for myself as I was with her. The climax came when I was hospitalized for pneumonia. At that point, my doctor told me enough was enough, and

that I had to get some help with my mother or I would die
before she did.

Unfortunately, it's all too easy to feel guilty about taking care of yourself when your parents are so needy. If you struggle with guilt, keep two things in mind. First, as Cora's case illustrates, you must take care of yourself in order to adequately care for someone else. If you're emotionally and/or physically drained, you need care yourself. And it's impossible to provide adequate care to another when you're personally spent.

The second thing to keep in mind is your own parenting experience. As a parent, would you want your child to suffer emotionally and physically as a result of taking care of you? No, you'd probably do whatever you could to protect your child from such damage. Assume that your parent feels the same about you. The worst thing that could happen to your parent would be to die thinking that he or she had brought physical and emotional harm to your life. In sum, taking care of yourself will also benefit your parent.

Maintaining an I–Thou Relationship

Philosopher Martin Buber distinguished between I–Thou and I–It relationships. In an I–Thou relationship you treat the other as a person, with dignity; you enter into a creative relationship with someone whom you respect as an individual of value. In an I–It relationship, you relate to the other as an object or a thing to be used or manipulated. You do not respect the other's individuality and value as a unique person (Buber 1937).

It is important to the well-being of both you and your parent that you strive to maintain an I–Thou relationship when you give care. You will feel far better about yourself and your relationship with your parent when you have treated your parent with dignity and respect. And your parent will be able to retain dignity in a painful situation.

It won't be easy to maintain the I–Thou relationship. Caregiving can easily deteriorate into an I–It relationship when you are exhausted or severely pressed for time, and when your parent suffers from a debilitating disease that makes him or her unable to respond or interact like other people. The following two cases show the difference between an I–Thou and an I–It caregiving situation. You will also realize the value of maintaining an I–Thou relationship.

First, the I–It relationship. Katie, a mother being cared for by her adult daughter, complained to us about her daughter's efforts to control her life:

She tells me what food I should eat. She tells me what television programs I should watch. She tells me when I need to go to bed at night and when I need to take a nap during the day. She even tells me how to vote. Sometimes I feel like my life is nothing more than following my daughter's instructions. Just because I am dependent on her now in ways we'd never anticipated doesn't mean I need to be treated like a child.

In this case, Katie's daughter related to her in an I–It fashion because of time pressures. Her daughter's work and other activities led her to minimize the time she gave to her mother. Katie's daughter didn't feel that she had enough time to allow her mother the dignity of making her own decisions. As a result, much of their mother-daughter interaction was an I–It relationship.

In contrast, Bart had a more positive experience with his father when he was in a nursing home:

My dad was a proud man. A severe stroke left him unable to talk and in need of professional care. He was angry and depressed about being put in the home. For a long time, he wouldn't cooperate with anyone. The nurses scolded him. My mother scolded him. I scolded him. It didn't help. Finally, one day I went to see him alone. Instead of scolding him, I sat and talked to him like I would have before he got sick. He could only shake his head yes or no, but we chatted for a while. I explained why it was necessary for him to be there, and I assured him of our love. And after a bit I asked him if he could help us all out by cooperating with the staff. He nodded yes. And he smiled at me in a loving way that I had not seen for months.

Bart's father responded positively to the I–Thou mode of relating. When his son talked *with* him instead of *at* him, he clearly felt he'd been treated with respect and dignity. He was a person again, not just a flawed body.

Accepting Your Limitations

There are some things you cannot do for your parents. You may be unable to give them all the care they need physically and emotionally. You may not have the skills or the equipment necessary to care properly for them. It's important for you to be aware of what you *cannot* do for your parents as well as what you can do, and then to accept your limitations. Don't allow feelings of guilt or inadequacy to hinder you. If you feel guilty, or you feel badly about yourself for being inadequate to the tasks, use self-talk such as the following:

- No one can do everything.

- I have to accept my limitations lest I do harm to my parents by trying to do what I cannot do properly.

- I love my parents even if I can't do all I would like for them.

- My task is to make sure my parents have the best care, not to give all that care myself.

Once you accept your limitations, you may have to draw on other resources to help. We'll discuss some of those resources in the succeeding section. Here we want to address the question of a nursing home or care facilities (which can either be temporary arrangements or final residences). For most people, it's one of the most difficult decisions to make. It forces the child to face his or her caregiving limitations. In addition, the needy parent may resist and resent the move.

Basically, there is one question to answer about the issue of placing your parent in a care facility: *Are you able*—in terms of time, physical and emotional strength, skills, and whatever other help you can bring in—*to give your parent the care that he or she needs*? If you answer "no," some kind of care facility is required.

If you place your parent in a facility, you'll need to spend time helping him or her deal with the transition. Remember to maintain an I–Thou relationship, which includes talking with your parent about his or her feelings. Keep in mind that going into a facility, even if it is a temporary measure, involves certain losses:

- Independence

- Freedom to schedule one's own activities

- Living in a familiar place with familiar people around

- Involvement in valued activities

Recall how you react to losses in your life. Your parent will have some of the same reactions—anxiety, anger, resentment, and depression. With continued loving attention, however, their reactions will lessen. So don't let them throw you into guilt or depression. Remind yourself that you've acted in the best interests of your parent and that your parent is getting the kind of care that he or she needs.

Identifying and Using Your Resources

Even if you don't place your parent in some kind of care facility, you may need additional resources. Generally, most communities have a wide range of available resources. Libraries have books that can help you understand the nature of your parent's condition and how best to help him or her. Hospitals and other agencies have people who can come to the home and provide various services, including medical care, meal preparation, transportation to the doctor, and shopping for necessities. Respite programs offer caregivers time off from their responsibilities. Meals on Wheels provides hot meals for the aged. Finally, you can find numerous sources of help on the Internet. "The Wellness at Home" site is a good place to begin. You can find it at (www.wellnessjunction.com/wellhome.htm). If you want to consult additional sites, simply use your search engine with the words "sandwich generation."

A first question to ask when considering additional resources is who else should or can help? Frequently, the burden of caregiving falls on one child—usually a daughter. But if you have siblings, they should also help. If they live in another city, they can at least help defray the costs of outside services. Your adult children as well as close friends of your parent may not only be able but eager to offer some help.

The second question to ask is, *what other resources are available in the community?* Begin by calling local agencies on aging (these are usually listed under "local government services" in the telephone directory). Also check your local hospitals and social service agencies. In addition, a number of national organizations offer various kinds of information and assistance in locating help for those caring for an aged parent or other relative. Check your telephone directory to find a number for any of the following: Eldercare Locator; Alzheimer's Association; The National Alliance for Caregiving; The National Association for Area Agencies on Aging; or the American Association of Retired Persons. The latter group will send you a caregiver resource packet.

Reframing Your Caregiving as Reaching Out

We suggested that you reframe the experience of children returning to the nest as an opportunity for reaching out. You can do the same with care of a parent. Offering comfort and support to an infirm, aged person is a worthy act of reaching out. Bart put it well:

> *While I was caring for my father, I didn't have time to do other things. At first, I found that irritating. But I began to look at it as my mission for that time in my life. I don't regret a minute of the time I spent with him. I'm grateful that I could be there for him just the way he always was there for me.*

Reflecting and Planning

As you reflect on your parent's needs for care, write down anything that you feel uncomfortable doing or for which you feel ill-prepared or inadequate. If your parent has a chronic disease of some kind, think about the additional needs that he or she will have in the future. Note any future caregiving tasks that would make you feel uncomfortable or for which you feel ill-prepared or inadequate.

Can you meet some of those needs by getting prepared through reading or skill training? Do you believe you should meet some of those needs by going ahead with the tasks in spite of your discomfort?

Before finalizing your list of needs for which you can use outside resources, discuss the items with your spouse, a close friend, or another relative. Through this kind of discussion, you can reduce any guilt or tendency to berate yourself for not doing certain things. And you can determine what tasks you lack the necessary skills to handle or what tasks might be physically or emotionally destructive for you.

Once you have your final list, contact the agencies we suggested earlier. Get the help you need for now and find out about available help you might need in the future. If you have any lingering hesitation about using the resources, remind yourself that your major responsibility is to maintain an I–Thou relationship with your parent and to make sure that your parent receives the kind of care that he or she needs.

Epilogue

In Celebration

At one time, I thought the empty nest was like turning the lights off in your life. Now I realize it is more like turning new lights on and enjoying the view.

—Chuck, a sixty-year-old
father of three

12

Fifty Ways to Celebrate
Your Empty Nest

We think that you have something to celebrate. You've raised your children and now they are on their own. This is an achievement worth commemorating. But you also have new worlds to conquer and exciting adventures ahead of you. And this is another reason for a celebration.

To help you celebrate, we have come up with a list of possibilities. You have encountered some of them in previous chapters. Others are new. Some work better for married people, others work well whatever your marital status. Some may sound trivial or silly. Others may seem out of your financial reach or impractical even though they are appealing. Some may be things you're already doing or in which you're not interested. Others may be things you never thought much about but are willing to try.

In any case, the items we have included have two purposes: to give you some specific things you can do and to stimulate your thinking about ways to celebrate. Keep in mind that something that is otherwise trivial can take on an entirely different meaning if you're doing it specifically to celebrate your new life. And something that is out of your financial reach can be brought back within reach if you modify it.

So use the list as a starting place. And celebrate!

1. Take the trip you've always fantasized about.

2. Enroll in a class exploring something in which you're interested.

3. Throw a "new phase of life" party.

4. Try five new restaurants; find at least three with a cuisine you've not had before.

5. Go on a religious or spiritual retreat.

6. Give a gift to a favorite charity in the name of your children.

7. Fly a kite.

8. Start a reading project, such as reading all of the Pulitzer Prize or National Book Award novels.

9. Join a theater company—if you don't want to act, you can help with scenery or lighting or selling tickets.

10. Take your spouse or a friend out on a mystery date—tell him or her only how to dress and when to be ready.

11. Have an "aroma" party where you pass around different fragrances for guests to enjoy. Have a prize for the guest who identifies the most fragrances.

12. Buy a surprise gift for your spouse or a friend.

13. Start jogging or hiking.

14. Contact someone who's been important in your life and express your appreciation for him or her.

15. Take up bird-watching and learn the calls of different birds.

16. Try something you've never done before—oil painting, playing a musical instrument, attending the horse races, and so on.

17. Make a new friend.

18. Revitalize an old friendship.

19. Go away for the weekend to the nearest health spa.

20. Buy yourself something you've wanted for a long time.

21. Volunteer to tutor a child who needs help with schoolwork.

22. Exchange homes for a few weeks with someone who lives in another country.

23. Attend a marriage enrichment weekend.

24. Select one quality you don't like about yourself and set up a program to change it.

25. Identify a quality you would like to have as a part of your identity and set up a program to develop it.

26. Visit gardens and smell the different kinds of flowers.

27. Write a letter to your children, telling each of them why they are special to you.

28. Learn yoga.

29. Volunteer to collect funds for a local charity.

30. Get a massage.

31. Take a bath or shower with your spouse; make it the beginning of a special evening.

32. Take a cruise.

33. Plant your own herb garden.

34. Take up gourmet cooking.

35. Teach a skill you have to a young person.

36. Spend a day trying to think only about the experience of the moment—open all your senses to your world.

37. Clean out your closets.

38. Eat vegetarian for a week.

39. Visit someone who is lonely.

40. Buy yourself a hot tub.

41. Offer to baby-sit or house-sit for a young couple so that they can get away for a weekend.

42. Relive a treasured experience with your spouse.

43. Send flowers to a friend—just because you value the friendship.

44. Identify a spiritual goal and draw up a plan to reach it.

45. Forgive someone who has wronged you.

46. Send your spouse a love letter.

47. Join a book-discussion group.

48. Find a book or some tapes on mental health and incorporate the best suggestions into your own life.

49. Attend a concert.

50. Invite a few neighbors you don't know to your house for a cup of coffee or a glass of wine.

Celebrate!!

References

Aquilino, William S. 1996. "The Returning Adult Child and Parental Experience at Midlife." In Carol D. Ryff, and Marsha Mailick Seltzer, eds., *The Parental Experience in Midlife*. Chicago: The University of Chicago Press.

Aurelius, Marcus. 1961. *Meditations*. London: J.M. Dent and Sons.

Bart, Pauline M. 1971. "Depression in Middle-Aged Women." In V. Gornick and B.K Moran, eds., *Women in Sexist Society*. New York: Mentor.

Berne, Eric. 1964. *Games People Play*. New York: Grove Press.

Bowlby, John. 1973. *Attachment and Loss, Vol. II: Separation*. New York: Basic Books.

Buber, Martin. 1937. *I and Thou*. Edinburgh: T. & T. Clark.

Cox, Frank D. 1993. *Human Intimacy: Marriage, the Family and Its Meaning, Sixth Edition*. St. Paul, MN.: West Publishing Co.

Flaste, Richard. 1991. "Sidelined by Loneliness." *New York Times Magazine*, April 28.

Hightower, Eugene. 1990. "Adolescent Interpersonal and Familial Precursors of Positive Mental Health at Midlife." *Journal of Youth and Adolescence* 19:257–76.

Levant, Ronald F., and Gini Kopecky. 1996. *Masculinity Reconstructed: Changing the Rules of Manhood—At Work, in Relationships, and in Family Life*. New York: Plume.

Mahon, Noreen E., Adela Yarcheski, and Thomas J. Yarcheski. 1993. "Health Consequences of Loneliness in Adolescents." *Research in Nursing and Health* 16:23–31.

Meredith, George. 1968. *The Egoist*. New York: Penguin Books.

Olson, Patricia S. 1993. *And Suddenly They're Gone: What Parents Need to Know about the Empty Nest*. Boulder: Tiffany Press.

National Education Association. 1994. "Parenting Your Parents." *NEA Today* 12:27.

Palisi, Bartolomeo J., and Claire Canning. 1983. "Urbanism and Social Psychological Well-Being: A Cross-Cultural Test of Three Theories." *The Sociological Quarterly* 24:527–43.

Rice, F. Philip. *Intimate Relationships, Marriages, and Families*. Mountain View, Ca.: Mayfield Publishing Company.

Rubenstein, Carin, and Phillip Shaver. 1982. *In Search of Intimacy*. New York: Delacorte Press.

Seligman, Martin E. P. 1975. *Helplessness: On Depression, Development, and Death*. San Francisco: W.H. Freeman.

United States Bureau of the Census. 1997. *Statistical Abstract of the United States 1997*. Washington: United States Department of Commerce.

Waring, E. M., and Gordon J. Chelune. 1983. "Marital Intimacy and Self-Disclosure." *Journal of Clinical Psychology* 39:183–90.

Wharton, Edith. 1989. *The Custom of the Country*. New York: Penguin Books.

Whitehead, Alfred North. 1933. *Adventures of Ideas*. New York: Mentor Books.

More New Harbinger Titles

BECOMING A WISE PARENT FOR YOUR GROWN CHILD

This warm and practical guide helps you assess problems, gain some perspective about them, and speak up or take action in ways that will strengthen your relationship with your adult children.   *Item WISE Paperback, $12.95*

CLAIMING YOUR CREATIVE SELF

The inspiring stories of thirteen women who were able to keep in touch with their own creative spirit opens the door to new definitions of creativity, and to the kinds of transforming ideas that will change your life.   *Item CYCS $15.95*

SIX KEYS TO CREATING THE LIFE YOU DESIRE

Helps you learn how to build a sense of trust, acknowledge your accomplishments, stop comparing yourself to others, achieve closeness, stop doubting your competence, and identify a core purpose that will let you follow through on your dreams.   *Item KEY6 $19.95*

BEING, BELONGING, DOING
Balancing Your Three Greatest Needs

This inspiring new book by therapist Ron Potter-Efron invites us to reevaluate our priorities and explore practical ways of keeping the components of our lives integrated and in balance.   *Item BBD Paperback, $10.95*

DON'T TAKE IT PERSONALLY
The Art of Dealing with Rejection

Reveals the power of negative childhood messages and shows how to depersonalize responses, establish boundaries, and develop a new sense of self-acceptance and self-confidence.   *Item DOTA Paperback, $12.95*

ILLUMINATING THE HEART
Steps Toward a More Spiritual Marriage

Outlines steps that couples can take to examine fundamental beliefs, search for shared meaning and purpose, and reconnect to each other, their families, and the wider community.   *Item LUM Paperback, $13.95*

Call **toll-free 1-800-748-6273** to order. Have your Visa or Mastercard number ready. Or send a check for the titles you want to New Harbinger Publications, 5674 Shattuck Avenue, Oakland, CA 94609. Include $3.80 for the first book and 75¢ for each additional book to cover shipping and handling. (California residents please include appropriate sales tax.) Allow four to six weeks for delivery.

Prices subject to change without notice.

Some Other New Harbinger Self-Help Titles

Claiming Your Creative Self: True Stories from the Everyday Lives of Women, $15.95
Six Keys to Creating the Life You Desire, $19.95
Taking Control of TMJ, $13.95
What You Need to Know About Alzheimer's, $15.95
Winning Against Relapse: A Workbook of Action Plans for Recurring Health and Emotional Problems, $14.95
Facing 30: Women Talk About Constructing a Real Life and Other Scary Rites of Passage, $12.95
The Worry Control Workbook, $15.95
Wanting What You Have: A Self-Discovery Workbook, $18.95
When Perfect Isn't Good Enough: Strategies for Coping with Perfectionism, $13.95
The Endometriosis Survival Guide, $13.95
Earning Your Own Respect: A Handbook of Personal Responsibility, $12.95
High on Stress: A Woman's Guide to Optimizing the Stress in Her Life, $13.95
Infidelity: A Survival Guide, $13.95
Stop Walking on Eggshells, $14.95
Consumer's Guide to Psychiatric Drugs, $16.95
The Fibromyalgia Advocate: Getting the Support You Need to Cope with Fibromyalgia and Myofascial Pain, $18.95
Healing Fear: New Approaches to Overcoming Anxiety, $16.95
Working Anger: Preventing and Resolving Conflict on the Job, $12.95
Sex Smart: How Your Childhood Shaped Your Sexual Life and What to Do About It, $14.95
You Can Free Yourself From Alcohol & Drugs, $13.95
Amongst Ourselves: A Self-Help Guide to Living with Dissociative Identity Disorder, $14.95
Healthy Living with Diabetes, $13.95
Dr. Carl Robinson's Basic Baby Care, $10.95
Better Boundries: Owning and Treasuring Your Life, $13.95
Goodbye Good Girl, $12.95
Being, Belonging, Doing, $10.95
Thoughts & Feelings, Second Edition, $18.95
Depression: How It Happens, How It's Healed, $14.95
Trust After Trauma, $15.95
The Chemotherapy & Radiation Survival Guide, Second Edition, $14.95
Surviving Childhood Cancer, $12.95
The Headache & Neck Pain Workbook, $14.95
Perimenopause, $16.95
The Self-Forgiveness Handbook, $12.95
A Woman's Guide to Overcoming Sexual Fear and Pain, $14.95
Don't Take It Personally, $12.95
Becoming a Wise Parent For Your Grown Child, $12.95
Clear Your Past, Change Your Future, $13.95
Preparing for Surgery, $17.95
The Power of Two, $15.95
It's Not OK Anymore, $13.95
The Daily Relaxer, $12.95
The Body Image Workbook, $17.95
Living with ADD, $17.95
When Anger Hurts Your Kids, $12.95
The Chronic Pain Control Workbook, Second Edition, $17.95
Fibromyalgia & Chronic Myofascial Pain Syndrome, $19.95
Kid Cooperation: How to Stop Yelling, Nagging & Pleading and Get Kids to Cooperate, $13.95
The Stop Smoking Workbook: Your Guide to Healthy Quitting, $17.95
Conquering Carpal Tunnel Syndrome and Other Repetitive Strain Injuries, $17.95
An End to Panic: Breakthrough Techniques for Overcoming Panic Disorder, Second Edition, $18.95
Letting Go of Anger: The 10 Most Common Anger Styles and What to Do About Them, $12.95
Messages: The Communication Skills Workbook, Second Edition, $15.95
Coping With Chronic Fatigue Syndrome: Nine Things You Can Do, $13.95
The Anxiety & Phobia Workbook, Second Edition, $18.95
The Relaxation & Stress Reduction Workbook, Fourth Edition, $17.95
Living Without Depression & Manic Depression: A Workbook for Maintaining Mood Stability, $18.95
Coping With Schizophrenia: A Guide For Families, $15.95
Visualization for Change, Second Edition, $15.95
Angry All the Time: An Emergency Guide to Anger Control, $12.95
Couple Skills: Making Your Relationship Work, $14.95
Self-Esteem, Second Edition, $13.95
I Can't Get Over It, A Handbook for Trauma Survivors, Second Edition, $16.95
Dying of Embarrassment: Help for Social Anxiety and Social Phobia, $13.95
The Depression Workbook: Living With Depression and Manic Depression, $17.95
Men & Grief: A Guide for Men Surviving the Death of a Loved One, $14.95
When Once Is Not Enough: Help for Obsessive Compulsives, $14.95
Beyond Grief: A Guide for Recovering from the Death of a Loved One, $14.95
Hypnosis for Change: A Manual of Proven Techniques, Third Edition, $15.95
When Anger Hurts, $13.95

Call **toll free, 1-800-748-6273,** to order. Have your Visa or Mastercard number ready. Or send a check for the titles you want to New Harbinger Publications, Inc., 5674 Shattuck Ave., Oakland, CA 94609. Include $3.80 for the first book and 75¢ for each additional book, to cover shipping and handling. (California residents please include appropriate sales tax.) Allow two to five weeks for delivery.

Prices subject to change without notice.